KT-231-268

Policing and Technology

Policing Matters

Policing and Technology

Barrie Sheldon
Paul Wright

Series editors
P A J Waddington
Martin Wright

First published in 2010 by Learning Matters Ltd

British Library Cataloguing in Publication Data
A CIP record for this book is available from the British Library.

ISBN: 978 1 84445 592 8

This book is also available in the following ebook formats:

Adobe ebook   ISBN: 978 1 84445 693 2
EPUB   ISBN: 978 1 84445 692 5
Kindle   ISBN: 978 1 84445 987 2

Cover design by Toucan Graphic Design Ltd
Text design by Code 5 Design Associates Ltd
Project management by Diana Chambers
Typeset by Kelly Winter
Printed and bound in Great Britain by TJ International, Padstow, Cornwall

Learning Matters Ltd
33 Southernhay East
Exeter EX1 1NX
Tel: 01392 215560
info@learningmatters.co.uk
www.learningmatters.co.uk

All weblinks and web addresses in the book have been carefully checked prior to publication, but for up-to-date information please visit the Learning Matters website, www.learningmatters.co.uk.

FSC
Mixed Sources
Product group from well-managed
forests and other controlled sources
Cert no. SGS-COC-2482
www.fsc.org
© 1996 Forest Stewardship Council

Contents

1 Introduction: the impact of technology on policing

CHAPTER OBJECTIVES

By the end of this chapter you should be able to:

- describe some of the impacts that the growth and rapid development of technology have had on the police service;
- explain how the police service has grasped technological opportunities to respond to the demands of modern-day policing;
- appreciate how both government and the police service have developed strategies to tackle the problem of cyber-crime;
- analyse a number of issues related to the impact of technology on policing.

LINKS TO STANDARDS

This chapter provides opportunities for links with the following Skills for Justice, National Occupational Standards (NOS) for Policing and Law Enforcement 2008.

AE1.1 Maintain and develop your own knowledge, skills and competence.
HA1   Manage your own resources.
HA2   Manage your own resources and professional development.

Links to NOS will be provided at the start of each chapter; however, it should be noted that the NOS are subject to review and it is recommended that you visit the Skills for Justice website to check the currency of all the NOS provided: www.skillsforjustice-nosfinder.com.

Overview of chapters

Each chapter provides a number of tasks that will help to develop your knowledge and understanding of the subject matter and also give you ideas to develop themes for academic assignments. Access to the Internet will be required for completion of tasks and a number of case studies are provided to link theory with practice.

Chapter 2 provides a brief historical overview of the development of the World Wide Web, introducing a range of applications that provide the opportunity to use the Internet as an effective intelligence tool. It illustrates both the problems and successes that can be achieved with the use of Internet technology and how different online intelligence analysis techniques can be used together or separately for the detection, investigation and prevention of crime through prosecution, disruption and dismantlement.

Chapter 3 explains the processes that are required when investigating cyber-crime and highlights some of the problems that can be faced. It provides the opportunity to develop a skill base, to investigate the abuse of information technology (IT), and to present legal, ethical and professional standards that must be taken into consideration. It also highlights the evidence that might be sought in a wide range of computer crime or misuse investigations, including, but not limited to, theft of trade secrets, theft of or destruction of intellectual property, and electronic fraud.

Chapter 4 explores investigation and surveillance on the Internet and introduces a range of technology that is now used in online investigations. Internet forensics is also explained, and this is supplemented with practical advice that highlights the growth of public surveillance on the Internet and how this has impacted on investigations. The chapter also explores some of the issues involved in the use of the Internet as an investigative tool, and includes a section relating to digital intelligence and how it has shaped cyber-crime investigations.

The use of computer forensics is a relatively new discipline and Chapter 5 addresses the ever increasing use of computer forensics in combating crime. It provides an under-standing of the computer and its applications, as well as how to use them in an investigative role. Forensic analysis is explained and some practical advice is given on how to search computer storage media for evidence. The chapter explains how to face the challenge of understanding both intricate technologies and the principles and practices of serious hi-tech and e-crime investigation.

Chapter 6 explores the use of closed-circuit television (CCTV), which has become an essential tool for the police investigator. The growth of CCTV in towns and cities has been profound during the past decade, bringing new opportunities for the investigator. A range of CCTV technology is introduced and the legislation, policy and procedures that an investigator is required to follow when using CCTV evidence are explored. The implications of CCTV technology are considered from a human rights perspective, exploring the safeguards that have been adopted and the so-called 'Big Brother' approach.

A counterfeit is an imitation made with the intent to represent dishonestly its content or origins. The word 'counterfeit' mainly describes forgeries of currency or documents, but can also describe software, pharmaceuticals, watches, patent infringement, and copyright and trademark infringement. Chapter 7 explores the offences of counterfeiting and what part technology and the Internet play. It shows how to investigate such crimes from a technical aspect, and where digital and forensic evidence should be sought.

An array of technology is now available to assist the road traffic investigator and Chapter 8 explores the growing use of automatic number plate recognition (ANPR) and road safety cameras, raising a number of ethical issues concerning their use. Ranges of other traffic measures where innovative technological solutions have been adopted are also explored, such as accident investigation, traffic control and law enforcement.

Chapter 9 provides a historical perspective of the development of police communications and how technology has changed the face of policing. Technologies relating to call handling and deployment, the Police National Computer, digital radio, crime reporting, mobile data devices and crime mapping will be explored. The chapter also examines the growing access to technology within a police custody suite and its implications for the operational officer, custody staff and detainees. The use of CCTV, tape recording of interviews and video identification is also examined.

Finally, Chapter 10 considers and identifies potential issues that may shape the future of policing investigations through the development of technology.

Introduction

Technology

Technology plays an essential role in modern policing and provides the investigator with an array of opportunities to bring perpetrators of crime to justice effectively and assist with other key responsibilities, such as death and major incident investigations. It also plays an important role in providing effective and robust communications systems: traffic management; intelligence gathering and dissemination; and administrative solutions. Unfortunately, the criminal fraternity at all levels has quickly grasped cutting-edge technology. It is currently recognised as a problem to overcome when dealing with organised crime and terrorism, which have both become global phenomena in no small part due to technological innovation. The challenge for law enforcement is to keep abreast of technological developments and be in a position to respond by:

- developing knowledge and understanding of technology;

- providing the tools to enable investigators to tackle crime effectively and to deal with other investigative responsibilities;

- keeping pace with the criminal fraternity's use of sophisticated computer and Internet techniques.

This challenge does not come without a cost. New technology is expensive and within a competitive market it is quickly superseded by improved and more sophisticated technology. The police service is required to work within limited budgets and the introduction of new technology has to be managed very carefully as procurement processes can be lengthy, expensive and resource intensive. We shall explore this more in due course and will identify how these issues are managed on both a national and a local basis, highlighting some of the problems the police service has already faced.

Police legitimacy

Another dimension to consider is how the technology used within modern policing has an impact upon the general public. The philosophy of the modern police service is that we police with the consent of the public, and there is growing evidence that some of the technology being used could compromise the legitimacy of the police. This is what the director of the National Policing Improvement Agency (NPIA) had to say in 2008:

> we argue that factual questions about the effectiveness of new technologies in detecting and preventing crime should not be separated from ethical and social questions surrounding the impact which these technologies might have upon civil liberties or public support for the police.

> (Neyroud and Disley, 2008)

REFLECTIVE TASK

Make a list of some of the technologies that you already know are currently being used by the police and consider how some may compromise police legitimacy or, in other words, have the potential for the public to lose confidence in the police. Where you have identified potential conflicts, consider what checks and safeguards have or could be utilised to maintain a balance between the rights of an individual and those of the state, who have responsibility for criminal justice and safeguarding communities.

Challenges made by civil liberty groups and concerns raised by members of the public will be explored in later chapters. For example, the controversial use of CCTV surveillance (Chapter 6) and the use of road safety cameras (Chapter 8) are both issues that have created public concern.

Cyber-crime

Cyber-crime, which is also referred to as computer crime, hi-tech crime, e-crime and electronic crime, involves unlawful activity where a computer, network or system is the subject, target or location of, or facilitates, a crime. The terms are interchangeable and all will be referred to throughout this book; however, in the main we will use the term cyber-crime. Whatever word is used, it has no boundaries in relation to global jurisdiction. Criminally, we have no *corpus juris*; in other words, we all have different legal systems, and in civil law we have no data harmonisation.

For the modern investigator cyber-crime has escalated to an unknown scale, growing out of all proportion, and policing worldwide has had to respond with strategies to tackle it. The credit crunch has contributed to increasing cyber-crime levels and the following statistics relating to the UK (Fafinski and Minassian, 2009, p3) were provided in September 2009:

- 3.6 million criminal acts committed online in 2008;

- account takeovers by fraudsters have risen by 207 per cent;

- online banking fraud is up by 132 per cent at a cost of £52.5 million.

The authors of the report highlight the difficulty in obtaining accurate crime figures and suggest that official crime statistics represent only the tip of the iceberg, and that cyber-crime is massively under-reported (Fafinski and Minassian, 2009, p23).

Investigative work can be costly and complex, demanding a high level of skill to obtain evidence and bring perpetrators to justice. The operational police officer will face daily challenges to deal with reports of cyber-crime and will often have to refer certain cases to specialists or other agencies to progress a criminal investigation. However, the Internet does provide opportunities for the investigation of crime and some useful tips and instruction will be provided in this book.

Historical perspective

The modern police service (1829 onwards) initially had the use of very simplistic equipment, such as the whistle, the truncheon and handcuffs, for communication, arrest of felons and personal protection. Significant scientific and technological developments have taken place in the twentieth century that have changed the face of policing. Table 1.1 provides some examples of how technology has developed considerably and how it is now shaping the way the police service conducts its business, including the core role of investigation.

Many more examples could be provided across the whole range of policing activity, with no area escaping the implications of technological development.

Table 1.1 The development of technology and its use by the police

The old	The new
Rattles and whistles	Sophisticated national digital radio service for the emergency services (Airwave)
Truncheon, handcuffs and a uniform with no protective capacity	Side-handled batons, CS incapacity spray, taser gun, quick cuffs, and protective vests with both knife and ballistic capability
Signal boxes, morse code, telegraphy, wireless and telex	Third-generation mobile phones, Internet, video conferencing
Locally based manual systems for collation and dissemination of intelligence	Local and national networked IT systems, providing immediate access to timely and detailed information (IMPACT)
Manual card systems for management of major investigations	IT system (HOLMES 2), providing automated incident, casualty, exhibit and disclosure management
Manual checking of fingerprint records	National automated fingerprint system, providing immediate results including a mobile live scan system (NAFIS)
Resource-intensive identification parades using volunteers from general public	Automated video identification parades (VIPER)

continued

Table 1.1 Continued

The old	The new
Radio centres providing cumbersome links to police wireless cars	Fully automated control centres having immediate access to a whole range of readily available intelligence and information, and automated links with other emergency services and key agencies for incident management
Manual vehicle checks, questioning of drivers, and document production	ANPR, where a camera linked to a database automatically reads registration numbers and immediately provides officers with vehicle status, ownership, warnings and document details

PRACTICAL TASK

Surrey Police have an excellent online interactive website for their museum of policing at www.surrey.police.uk/museum/default.asp. Find the virtual museum; select the 'Topics' link and then select the 'Communications' link by clicking on the police radio. Work your way through the section and discover how technology has developed and enhanced the communications capability of Surrey Police. Consider how improved communications may be of benefit to the investigator. (This issue will be discussed further in Chapter 9.)

CASE STUDY

The following provides an example of how crime was recorded within Staffordshire prior to the turn of the new century.

A police officer would attend the scene of a crime and take a written statement from the victim. Details from the statement would then be used to write out a crime report. The officer was then required to return to the police station, where the details of the crime would be written into an 'Occurrence book' for the information of other officers. In some police stations the details of the crime then had to be sent by telex to other police stations and departments. The crime report and statement would then go to an administration department to be further recorded on other systems and then to a supervisor for checking, allocation and further instruction.

Let's now compare this with what is happening today. Many of our crimes are reported directly to crime reporting centres where the details are entered immediately on to automated systems in which recording, distribution and circulation can be achieved at the press of a button. Further, the use of mobile data devices (see Chapter 9) is now having considerable impact on policing, with technology becoming available to enable officers to take crime reports and statements at the scene of a crime and send them online to administrative units for automated recording and processing, with the added bonus of providing real-time information for operational officers and police managers.

Police science and technology organisations

As the reliance on both science and technology has increased, a number of organisations have become responsible for procurement, development and advising the police service on science and technology. Substantial government funding is provided for these services, which are critical in ensuring that the police service and other law enforcement agencies are able to respond effectively to scientific and technological advances. However, at the same time, spending must be focused and aligned to national criminal justice priorities. The following provides a brief overview of some of the organisations concerned.

Home Office Science and Research Group

The Home Office is organisationally divided into a number of directorates. The Science and Research Group (SRG) is a directorate that is further divided into five groups:

- Animal (Scientific Procedures) Division;

- Home Office Scientific Development Branch (HOSDB);

- Research Development and Statistics;

- Science and Research Group Support;

- Science Secretariat.

(We shall be focusing on the role of the HOSDB. Information regarding the other four units can be found online at www.homeoffice.gov.uk/about-us/organisation/directorate-search/srg/index.html.)

Police Scientific Development Branch

The Police Scientific Development Branch (PSDB) was introduced by the Home Office during the 1960s to provide advice to government and the police service on science and technology techniques and equipment. The group attracted considerable funding and has developed many policing technological solutions, such as covert surveillance, ballistics protection, and road policing technologies. The PSDB was replaced by the HOSDB.

Home Office Scientific Development Branch

The HOSDB is made up of teams of scientists and engineers who provide advice, delivery and implementation of effective operational solutions for the Home Office and its partners, such as the police service, on any issue relating to science and technology. The teams are based at two sites in Sandridge, Hertfordshire and Langhurst, West Sussex. The HOSDB assists the Home Office in meeting their strategic objectives relating to policing, crime reduction, counter terrorism, border security and identity management.

Forensic Science Service

The Forensic Science Service (FSS) is the principle provider of forensic services to the police service. It became an executive agency of the Home Office in 1991, merging with the Metropolitan Police forensic science laboratory in 1996, and became government owned in 2005. Besides providing forensic services, it is also involved with the development and deployment of new and advanced scientific techniques.

Forensic Science Regulator

The Forensic Science Regulator is a public appointee whose role is to ensure that the provision of forensic science services across the criminal justice system is subject to an appropriate regime of scientific quality standards.

Police Information Technology Organisation

The Police Information Technology Organisation (PITO) was established in 1996 and was given the responsibility of managing national information technology and communications development for the police service. Some examples of the technologies it worked on included call handling, case and custody management, the Violent and Sex Offender Register (ViSOR), Airwave, and the Home Office Large Major Enquiry System (HOLMES 2). In 2007, PITO ceased as an organisation and became part of the NPIA.

National Policing Improvement Agency

Following the Police and Justice Act 2006, the NPIA was introduced on 1 April 2007 with a remit of ensuring that agreed programmes of police reform were implemented. The new agency centralised certain police services, including PITO (see above) and the Central Police Training and Development Authority (CPTDA, commonly known as CENTREX), and now takes the lead on a range of key scientific and technological projects for the police service.

PRACTICAL TASK

Find the NPIA website at www.npia.police.uk and identify the range of scientific and technological projects for which it is currently responsible.

Home Office strategy: science and technology

The Home Office produced its first *Police Science & Technology Strategy* in January 2003, promising to equip the police service with the best tools and techniques available to maximise police efficiency and effectiveness. At this time, police reform was beginning to gather momentum and a national policing plan had been produced for the first time, outlining a number of key policing priorities that included tackling antisocial behaviour, volume crime such as burglary and car crime, serious organised crime, and drugs.

The strategy was necessary to ensure that funding and developmental priorities for both science and technology was aligned to the national policing priorities. A Police Science and Technology Strategy Group was introduced in July 2002, made up of representatives from the Home Office, the Association of Chief Police Officers (ACPO), the Association of Police Authorities (APA), key agencies such as the FSS, PITO and PSDB, and other agencies, including independent organisations such as the Royal Academy of Engineering.

PRACTICAL TASK

Go to http://dircweb.king.ac.uk/vitab/documents/police_science_and_technology_strategy_2003-2008.pdf and download the Police Science & Technology Strategy 2003–2008. Go to appendix 4 (page 23) and read through the range of projects and technologies under development at that time and identify how some of those projects were intended to benefit the police investigator.

You may have been surprised about the extent and range of technologies under development, many of which are now in use or in the latter stages of development, providing essential tools for a police investigator.

The cost of technology has already been mentioned as an issue and, in 2003, the police service spent £900 million on science and technology products and services. A further £334 million was spent on the DNA expansion programme, Airwave, the National Strategy for Police Information Systems (NSPIS), national projects, and research and development. A staggering total of £1.23 billion (Home Office, 2003, p22) evidences a huge commitment by government to enhance the effectiveness of the police service and tackle crime through the use of science and technology.

The government currently has a three-year *Science and Innovation Strategy 2009–12* (Home Office, 2009b), with six priority areas:

- cross-cutting priorities that support all business areas of the Home Office;
- crime;
- policing;
- identity management;
- border control and migration;
- security and counter-terrorism.

Government and cyber-crime

The Government is committed to action against hi-tech crime in line with our objective of making the UK the best and safest place in the world to conduct and engage in e-commerce.

(Straw, 2000)

Just as in the 19th century we had to secure the seas for our national safety and prosperity, and in the 20th century we had to secure the air, in the 21st century we also have to secure our advantage in cyber space.

(Home Office, 2009a, p5)

The second quotation above is taken from the government's *Cyber Security Strategy* and makes it quite clear that cyber-security has become a national security issue. The government, public sector organisations, businesses and individuals are now very reliant on cyberspace, and any disruption would cause a major national crisis, confusion and chaos. For the terrorist, in particular, cyberspace provides a new area for attacks, and criminals worldwide are already exploiting cyberspace to carry out a whole range of unlawful activities.

To put the national security issue in perspective, the following list (Home Office, 2009a, p12) provides some examples of key services that could be severely disrupted following a major cyberspace attack:

- power supply;
- food distribution;
- water supply and sewerage;
- financial services;
- broadcasting;
- transportation;
- health;
- emergency, defence and government services.

To help protect the UK against electronic attack, the Centre for the Protection of the National Infrastructure (CPNI) has been established and provides protective security advice to businesses and organisations across the national infrastructure. Examples of the security advice that the CPNI provides (CPNI, 2010) are to:

- assess the risks to your business;
- consider security first when planning building works;
- establish a security culture in your business;
- keep premises clear and tidy;
- control access points and use staff and visitor passes;
- install physical measures, e.g. locks, alarms, CCTV and lighting;
- establish good mail-handling procedures;
- recruit carefully, checking identities and following up references;
- take proper IT security precautions;
- test your business continuity plans regularly.

Go to www.cabinetoffice.gov.uk/media/216620/css0906.pdf and download the current Cyber Security Strategy. Focus on chapter 3, pages 15–20, and read how the government proposes to tackle cyberspace security. The approach is multifaceted, involving a cross-section of organisations. Identify the three strategic aims and associated objectives, and then analyse the approaches being adopted and consider how effective they are likely to be.

From this last task you will have noted that the police have a specific responsibility for e-crime and have produced a strategy that defines and scopes the national response of the police service (see below).

E-Crime Unit of the Serious Organised Crime Agency

The National Hi-Tech Crime Unit (NHTCU) was introduced in April 2001 and was the UK's first dedicated squad to tackle cyber-crime. The unit was based in London and was made up of staff from the police service, Her Majesty's Customs and Excise (HMCE), the Royal Air Force and specialised personnel from the private sector.

In April 2006, the NHTCU became the e-Crime Unit of the newly formed Serious Organised Crime Agency (SOCA), which brought the National Crime Squad (NCS), National Criminal Intelligence Service (NCIS), and parts of the investigative arms of the Customs, Inland Revenue and Immigration services together. However, despite evidence of the escalating problem of cyber-crime, the availability of local services for reporting and investigating it became limited as a result of this change.

This problem was highlighted in a *Science and Technology* report published by the House of Lords in July 2007, which made a number of recommendations relating to the policing of the Internet, including:

- the development of a unified web-based reporting system for e-crime;

- the police service to devote more resources to the investigation of e-crime;

- the establishment of a network of computer forensic laboratories;

- the establishment of a Police Central e-Crime Unit, with the government taking responsibility for providing appropriate financing.

This report paved the way for the development of a policing e-crime strategy.

ACPO e-Crime Strategy

ACPO published their first *e-Crime Strategy* in May 2009 and provided a definition for e-crime:

> *The use of networked computers or Internet technology to commit or facilitate the commission of crime.*

> (ACPO, 2009, p2)

The strategy (ACPO, 2009, p4) outlines six objectives, which are to:

- nationally reduce the harm caused by e-crime;

- increase national mainstream capability to deal with e-crime across the police service;

- coordinate a national approach to e-crime;

- prevent e-crime, and make it more difficult to commit;

- improve the national investigative capability for the most serious e-crime incidents;

- develop and capitalise partnership engagement with industry, academia, law enforcement and government, both domestically and internationally.

The strategy promises much and, if achieved, it will be good news for both the general public and law enforcement investigators. From your own experience it is likely that you have been a victim of cyber-crime in some form, such as a 'phishing' or 'obfuscated URL' attack, where you may have received an unsolicited email informing you that there is a problem with your bank account and that you need to click on a link within the message to rectify the problem. The link will take you to a bogus, but authentic-looking, web page that will ask you to enter personal information. This data will then be used to facilitate or commit online and 'real-world' fraud. Every message received is an attempted fraud, but most are not reported unless there is an actual loss and, even when reported, the police often do not have the necessary resources to complete an effective investigation.

ACPO recognised that many victims of e-crime did not know how or to whom an e-crime should be reported. Some people, and in particular businesses, are reluctant to report e-crimes because they want to reduce reputational damage and financial loss. In addition, they want to maintain control of any such investigation and some believe that the police do not have the capability to investigate e-crime. The National Fraud Reporting Centre (NFRC), managed by the City of London Police, has been identified as a national reporting centre for e-crime.

Some of the proposed benefits of the ACPO strategy (ACPO, 2009, p5) include:

- increasing the skills of specialist officers who investigate e-crime;

- mainstreaming e-crime into everyday policing and law enforcement activities;

- improving public confidence in both the police's and law enforcement agencies' ability to effectively record and investigate instances of e-crime.

Police Central e-Crime Unit

Funding for the Police Central e-Crime Unit (PCeU) was provided by both the government (£3.5 million) and the Metropolitan Police (£3.9 million) for a three-year period from 2008–09. The PCeU was introduced in October 2008 and is based at New Scotland Yard, London, with a threefold mission to:

- improve the police response to the victims of e-crime;

- coordinate the law enforcement approach to all types of e-crime;

- provide a national investigative capability for the most serious e-crime incidents.

(adapted from Metropolitan Police, 2010)

C H A P T E R   S U M M A R Y

Within this chapter we have briefly considered the impact science and technology have had on both the government and policing, with a particular focus on cyber-crime, which will be explored further as you progress through this book.

Police investigation has changed dramatically in recent times, with both science and technology providing new challenges for society, new opportunities for investigators, and, unfortunately, a world of opportunity for criminals.

Innovations such as the science of DNA; forensic examination of computers and mobile phones; and CCTV and ANPR have considerably changed traditional investigative policing practices.

New government and policing strategies have been introduced during 2009 and it is not yet known how effective they will be and what impact they will have on the public's confidence in the police's ability to tackle cyber-crime, reduce crime and create safer communities.

The tasks completed will have provided you with further information and resources to assist with your studies and have opened up some areas for debate. The content of this chapter is limited, providing you with a brief overview of government and policing strategies, structures and some issues relating to investigation. Further reading and research should help in building on some of the information presented.

REFERENCES

Association of Chief Police Officers (ACPO) (2009) *ACPO e-Crime Strategy*. London: ACPO.

Centre for the Protection of the National Infrastructure (CPNI) (2010) Top ten security guidelines. Available online at www.cpni.gov.uk (accessed 18 January 2010).

Fafinski, Stefan and Minassian, Neshan (2009) *UK Cyber-crime Report 2009*. Richmond: Garlik UK. Available online at www.garlik.com/cyber-crime_report.php (accessed 15 January 2010).

Home Office (2003) *Police Science & Technology Strategy 2003–2008*. London: Home Office Science Policy Unit.

Home Office (2009a) *Cyber Security Strategy of the United Kingdom: Safety, security and resilience in cyber space*. London: The Stationery Office.

Home Office (2009b) *Science and Innovation Strategy 2009–12*. London: Home Office Science and Research Group.

House of Lords (2007) *Select Committee Science and Technology: Fifth report.* online at: www.publications.parliament.uk/pa/ld200607/ldselect/ldsctech/165/16502.htm (accessed 13 January 2010).

Metropolitan Police (2010) *PCeU Police Central e-Crime Unit*. Available online at www.met.police.uk/pceu/index.htm (accessed 13 January 2010).

Neyroud, Peter and Disley, Emma (2008) Technology and policing: implications for fairness and legitimacy. *Policing: A Journal of Policy and Practice*, 2(2): 226–32.

Straw, Jack (2000) Quoted in Government launches £25 million initiative against cybercrime. Outlaw.com, 14 November. Available online at www.out-law.com/page-1159 (accessed 29 January 2010).

USEFUL WEBSITES

All weblinks and web addresses in the book have been carefully checked prior to publication, but for up-to-date information please visit the Learning Matters website, www.learningmatters.co.uk.

http://scienceandresearch.homeoffice.gov.uk (Home Office Science, Research and Statistics)

www.acpo.police.uk (Association of Chief Police Officers)

www.cpni.gov.uk (Centre for the Protection of the National Infrastructure)

www.met.police.uk (Metropolitan Police)

www.npia.police.uk (National Policing Improvement Agency)

Police and Justice Act 2006

2 The Internet and intelligence

CHAPTER OBJECTIVES

By the end of this chapter you should be able to:

- understand the relationship between intelligence and the Internet;
- describe how the Internet works;
- appreciate that there are sources of information and intelligence freely available on the Internet;
- establish efficient and effective online investigative strategies in relation to the gathering of digital information and intelligence;
- recognise the online tools that can be used to gather information and intelligence.

LINKS TO STANDARDS

National Occupational Standards (NOS) describe competent performance in terms of outcomes. With a clear assessment strategy, developed in parallel with the standards, they allow a comprehensible assessment of competence aligned with nationally agreed standards of performance. In this way, they define what has to be achieved, rather than what has to be done.

The Association of Chief Police Officers (ACPO) has signed up to National Occupational Standards (developed by Skills for Justice) and in December 2006 the NOS for countering e-crime were introduced. The following refer to those standards that specifically relate to digital intelligence and cyber-crime.

CO1   Identify and secure electronic evidence sources.
CO2   Seize and record electronic evidence sources.
CO3   Capture and preserve electronic evidence.
CO4   Investigate electronic evidence.
CO5   Evaluate and report electronic evidence.
CO6   Conduct Internet investigations.
CM101 Develop, apply and share knowledge in your specialist area.
CM102 Obtain and analyse information for intelligence purposes.

Introduction

The aim of this chapter is to give the reader an understanding of how the Internet is constructed and to give you, the investigator, the knowledge of how efficient and effective online searches can be achieved.

We will cover the collection of cyber-crime intelligence related to both the crime under investigation and those crimes that may be discovered as a consequence. We will show that agencies need to produce robust procedures that encompass the recommendations made by authorities, noting that online products and services that can assist criminals to commit crime are surprisingly unregulated in cyberspace.

The Internet

What is the Internet? The Internet is the world's largest computer network and it has developed quickly over recent years. It began life as an experimental network used and controlled by academics to share information and encourage professional communication between organisations. Within this framework, self-governance worked well because the community of users shared common goals. Now it has evolved into a public domain, where anyone can share and access this common resource.

Intranet and extranet

An intranet is a private computer network that is enclosed within an organisation. It uses Internet technologies to share the organisation's information and resources securely with its employees.

An extranet is a private network that uses Internet protocols, network connectivity, and the public telecommunications system to share part of an organisation's information or resources securely with trusted third parties or other businesses. It can be classed as an element of an organisation's intranet that is extended to others beyond the organisation.

The World Wide Web

The most widely used and recognised service available on the Internet is the World Wide Web (WWW), also known as 'the web'. It can be described as a set of electronic documents that are linked together like an intricate network. These documents are stored on computers called servers. It has now evolved into a worldwide electronic publishing site and, increasingly, a tool for conducting e-commerce, and as a consequence cyber-crime.

How the web works

As a consequence of the creation of the web, objects such as audio and computer graphics are incorporated with text into a single item that can be communicated globally. These items are referred to as HTML documents, or web pages. Hypertext Mark-up Language (HTML) enables different types of computers to read the same files without first converting the files to the format of the different application software that supports or improves the user's work. Within these HTML files, specific words or images serve as links to other, separate files, allowing users to move easily from one web page or site to another. These text or graphic areas can be found by moving the mouse pointer over the link, which causes the pointer to change shape. HTML can link files stored on the same computer, or on other computers located around the globe. A compilation of web pages is known as a website.

PRACTICAL TASK

Internet crime is a growing phenomenon and world leaders continue to seek powers to access and control information generated on the Internet to prevent, reduce and detect crime. Monitoring of Internet use and the interception of communications such as emails are just two methods of obtaining potential intelligence or evidence, which, if used widely, could discourage online criminal activity.

Consider and write down a list of arguments for and against this type of approach to deter crime and consider the issues of privacy and proportionality.

Using the Internet as an investigative tool

The Internet continues to change society, from the way we communicate with each other, to how we find information and purchase a whole array of goods. All of these have changed drastically over the past few years as a direct result of the Internet.

The regular expansion of information, easily obtained by anyone with access to a computer and able to connect to the Internet, is incredible. Regrettably, not all of those who use the Internet do so with good intentions. There is a growing amount of information on the Internet that is showing the minority how to commit various unlawful acts using a computer and the Internet. Criminals are also able to communicate with absolute impunity by using freely available tools and applications to hide their identities and their communication channels.

The challenge for law enforcement and other investigative agencies is to understand how new technologies are associated with traditional crime. When the first motorcar was produced, criminals took full advantage of it while law enforcement agencies sat back and, in due course, had to catch up. Similarly, if the police service and partner organisations do not act now to tackle Internet crime effectively, the criminal fraternity once again will be one step ahead.

The Internet represents a significant investigative and cost-effective intelligence tool. The information it provides can prove very useful, as it can be accessed with relative ease by a proficient investigator.

A number of investigative search tools are available for the Internet, but they can be awkward. They may appear to be outwardly easy to use, but finding specific pieces of information can at times be easier said than done, and these tools may be intimidating due to their exclusive and significant limitations. Being able to handle the huge amounts of data returned from a comparatively simple keyword search can be overwhelming and time-consuming.

Building an armoury of the various Internet research tools available will play an important role in the development of valuable investigative analysis and research. Just as important will be the skill to understand, analyse and disseminate effectively the results of any Internet investigation; for example, who is the person or persons behind the data? Can the data be corroborated? How current is the information?

Cyber-crime affects most Internet users and the associated electronic intelligence and evidence can frequently be recovered by forensic examination (see Chapter 5), by analysis of computing equipment used by the offender or victim, and on occasions from the components of the Internet itself. Huge amounts of data can be recovered that need analysing by the investigator, and the care and storage of this information can present issues that impact upon the privacy of others. The advance of technology and the innovation of the criminal mind leave regulation and legislation trying to catch up. However, more and more investigators are gaining the necessary knowledge and awareness of what to ask of their Internet, network and forensic investigators.

Early liaison with the analyst can provide a number of benefits, including:

- identification of the type and scope of the technology being used;
- understanding of the significance of the Internet and digital activity to the investigation;
- knowledge of the use to which technology is being put by the offenders;
- identification of the areas of the Internet likely to hold valuable intelligence or evidence.

PRACTICAL TASK

It is vital to consider how the cyber-criminal uses the Internet and digital resources for intelligence purposes, noting that intelligence refers to information that provides knowledge in order that you can take or assess a different course of action.

Make a list of three different types of Internet site, for example a financial institution, a retail outlet, etc., that might be used by an organised crime group to gather information. Then explain what intelligence might be gained from each of these types of Internet site.

Data and information

When searching for information, one must be prepared to encounter problems in the following important areas: information volume, reliability and authenticity. At the same time, the investigator needs to differentiate between what is 'nice to know' and what is 'need to know' information. In addition, and in order to achieve this, one needs the appropriate resources and websites that can assist in such an undertaking.

Data, information and intelligence

Many people use the terms data and information as synonyms. There are differences, however, and these are fundamental to conducting an Internet investigation. Data consists of statements that, when corroborated, become fact, and these facts, when put together, provide information. Investigators are accustomed to gathering and reviewing all the available information. Intelligence results when information is analysed and interpreted. This is then graded as to the reliability of the source and the data/information itself. Utilising this definition, it is important to understand that data and information have little or no importance unless corroborated. The information is only valuable when it is interpreted and thus turned into intelligence.

Collective intelligence

A good example of this is the media, which is regularly associated with the use and improvement of collective intelligence. It has the ability to store and retrieve information effortlessly through the effective use of databases and the Internet. It is then able to facilitate the sharing of this information and intelligence with very little difficulty.

In this situation, collective intelligence is frequently confused with shared knowledge. The earlier is knowledge that is *available* to all members of a group, while the second is information that is *known* by all members of a group.

Tracing information

Locating the computer where the activity originated or is housed is usually the first goal towards solving an Internet-related crime or a case of computer abuse. Despite the availability of software tools to find it, such as NSLookup or Tracert, among others, the true source of an email or the host of a website is often hidden behind clouds of electronic smokescreens. For every tool to identify a computer, there seems to be another tool designed to hide it. The more technically competent the user is, the more difficult will be the investigation.

Each computer connected to the Internet is assigned a unique address known as an IP (Internet Protocol) address that can be *static* or *dynamic*. If you have a permanent connection to the Internet, you are highly likely to have a static address. Dynamic addresses are associated with dial-up connections and session connections. An investigator needs to be aware that this does change if you are part of a network that is connected to the Internet through a default gateway.

For the general public, such a gateway is usually the device provided by the Internet service provider (ISP) that connects their computers to the Internet. In organisations, the default gateway is commonly taken to be the node (communication endpoint) connecting the internal networks to outside networks and the Internet.

Intelligence cycle

The intelligence cycle (see Figure 2.1) is a useful model for considering how to convert information to intelligence that can then be used for a number of policing purposes in tackling crime, for example prevention, prosecution, disruption, dismantlement, disinformation, damage control and containment.

1. **Collection plan**: the Internet is a valuable source and, like any other intelligence interview, the interrogation needs to be well planned and well documented.

2. **Reconnaissance**: this is the preparatory phase – what needs to be asked and what areas of the source are likely to give results.

3. **Focus**: this will depend to a degree on the individual, investigative requirements and legislation, especially with regard to the Regulation of Investigatory Powers Act 2000 and the Criminal Procedure and Investigations Act 1996. The implications of these and other related legislation make it essential that an audit trail is kept, and if necessary can be revealed during a formal process. The Internet has no boundaries, unlike law enforcement that has physical and jurisdictional boundaries, so an investigator needs to be familiar with legislation that may impact on their actions in the UK and overseas.

4. **Footprinting**: this is the methodological mapping of a target or targets. It results in a unique profile of an individual or an organisation with respect to information and intelligence.

5. **Conduct**: at this point an evaluation report should be created listing the potential sources of information and/or intelligence.

6. **Corroboration**: this is essential to validate the data.

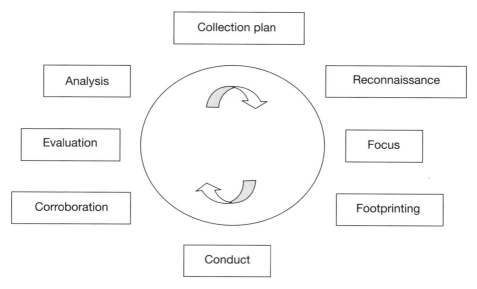

Figure 2.1 The intelligence cycle

7. **Evaluation**: the reliability and authenticity of data must take place against given criteria.

8. **Analysis**: this allows for data to be processed into graded information or intelligence.

The use of intelligence is an incomplete procedure that requires repetitive re-evaluation in order that any set objectives can be achieved. Each time new information and intelligence have been gathered, the process should start again.

REFLECTIVE TASK

The Internet is the online equivalent of a public place and there is a need to provide safety for those who use it, balanced against taking firm action against those who abuse it.

- *Should services and products be safe and protect users from harm and, if harm is caused, should the Internet provider be held responsible?*

- *Should the Internet provider be accountable for the preservation of information that may be of use for both intelligence and evidential purposes? Construct an argument for or against this proposal.*

PRACTICAL TASK

The Data Retention (EC Directive) Regulations 2009 now puts the responsibility on communication and Internet service providers to retain information for a period of 12 months.

These regulations have caused some controversy and debate, particularly from civil liberty organisations. Go to the following two links online and discover what was said in Parliament when the regulations were approved, and then compare this against the comments made by the civil liberty group.

- *www.theyworkforyou.com/lords/?id=2009-03-24a.620.0 (House of Lords debate 24 March 2009)*

- *www.liberty-human-rights.org.uk/pdfs/policy08/comms-data-directive.pdf*

Now compare your findings with the argument you constructed for the previous task and decide whether government has the balance right between freedom and security. This argument could form the basis of an assignment topic when exploring Internet crime.

Internet searching and browsers

Browsers are programs that allow the user access to the web. They are software applications that are used for retrieving and producing digital resources. This has led some to describe the web browser as the 'universal platform'.

The web didn't really take off until the release of Netscape Navigator, which created new browser and web page standards, such as tables and frames. Microsoft came into the game more with Internet Explorer (IE), spurring the competition known as the 'browser wars', but also encouraging innovation. There are now a number of general browsers available for the Internet and they all work in a similar way. IE 8 is the latest Microsoft version; it portrays itself as being faster, easier and safer than ever. It has a number of security enhancements that give the user trustworthy browsing, which means that, as more privacy features are added and, at times, demanded, there is less information and intelligence to be recovered.

Browser workings

The browser is the 'front end' programme that allows the user to access most Internet facilities. The browser will record and store a great deal of information about the user's online activity in what is known as *index.dat* files – .dat is a filename extension for a number of different types of data files. The type of information available includes details of the sites that a user has accessed, as well as details of visits to newsgroups, websites, chatrooms and certain emails. Fortunately, by getting the most out of a web browser, the user leaves forensic artefacts. Other web-based programs can also generate entries.

Chat applications use Hypertext Transfer Protocol (HTTP) sessions to maintain connections between the server (source of information) and the client (user), and to regularly update the web page. After a specific interval, a 'reload' request from the user's web browser will be sent to the chat server. The operation is carried out completely without the knowledge of the user, who would only interact with the chat page. It is possible to reconstruct some of these live chat HTML pages and, therefore, we have potential intelligence and/or evidence. The user may well be unaware that this information has been retained by their computer.

Browser data

An Internet history list is present to make it easy for the user to find and return to websites and pages visited. It does not matter whether it was today or a few days ago, the list can record every page the user visited. Most current browsers record the web pages visited today, yesterday and beyond. The user sees these organised in folders by the date visited, and each page visited on that given site set out in alphabetical order.

History settings can be found in 'User configurable', which can be accessed by selecting 'Tools' on the menu bar when in IE and then selecting 'Internet options', and then 'Browser history settings'. These settings can range from a minimum of 0 days to a maximum of 999 days, with the default usually set at 20 days.

A file is located on a user's hard disk in which a browser stores the website data for every web page or Uniform Resource Locator (URL – see explanation below) address that a user visits. When the web server sends the web page files to the browser, they are stored in a file, so that the next time the user visits the same website the browser takes the data from the temporary Internet file. With this method, the page quickly displays in the browser instead of the user having to wait for a response from the website's server all over again.

The browser is opening the web page from the user's hard drive instead of downloading the files from the Internet, which serves to increase the perceived browsing speed.

Cookies are text files deposited on a computer's hard drive by the browser after visiting a website that uses them. Each has a different format, and they contain certain information so that the site can recognise the user on their return. The user's browser writes the cookie to a system, and does so at the request of the web developer.

Linking

The main power of HTML comes from its ability to link text and/or an image to another page or section of a page. A browser highlights the identified text or image with colour and/or underlines to indicate that it is a hypertext link, which is often shortened to 'hyperlink' or just 'link'. When you click on a link in an HTML document, your web browser is actually sending a request to download a file stored on a remote computer. When you click on a link on a website, to go to another, the new one does not send a cookie.

PRACTICAL TASK

A person with a small amount of knowledge can locate and view the history of almost all a computer's activities; however, a user can restrict what is recorded. Go to the 'User configurable' settings on your own computer (i.e., select 'Tools' while on a web page) and explore the tabs under 'Internet options'. Within the 'General' tab:

- *change your homepage to 'http://www.google.co.uk';*

- *delete temporary Internet files and cookies in the browsing history section;*

- *in the same section, select 'Settings' and change the default setting of history from 20 to 1 day.*

What is a URL?

As mentioned previously, browser software uses URLs to locate files on the web. The information in an URL gives the user the capability to jump from one page or website on the web to another with relative ease. However, the web is just one part of the Internet. The user's web browser can also access other parts of the Internet by using URLs that characterise other types of Internet data and services.

Anatomy of a URL

The URL consists of a unique numbering system that looks like a telephone number, such as 64.74.98.80. These numbers can be difficult to remember, so a domain name system (DNS) is used to convert the numeric address to a text version, therefore making it easier to read and remember.

Proxies

On occasions, web browsers will not interact directly with a web server, they will go via a proxy. HTTP proxies are used to reduce network traffic, allow access through firewalls and provide content filtering, and more. The proxy works by forwarding a request to a web server and retrieving the responses, in other words acting like a client. Then it completes the cycle by returning the response to the client. It is possible for a single HTTP request to pass through multiple proxies.

PRACTICAL TASK

- *Find out about the anatomy of URLs by accessing www.teachersfirst.com/tutorial/ url-new.shtml.*

- *Identify how this may help you with both academic and investigative research.*

Search engines

A search engine is a tool designed to search for information, the results of which are normally displayed in a list and are referred to as 'hits'. The information produced may consist of web pages, images, text and other types of files. A number of search engines also mine data that is present in databases or open directories.

The Internet represents an important investigative tool and an unprecedented, cost-effective 'open source' intelligence-gathering opportunity. This is information that could prove very useful in many types of cyber-crime investigations, and can be accessed with relative ease by an experienced and proficient Internet researcher or forensic analyst.

Search engines can be awkward in that, while they may appear to be seemingly easy to use, finding specific pieces of information and intelligence can be tricky and disheartening due to their user restrictions. Dealing with and analysing the large amounts of data returned from a straightforward query can be very time-consuming.

Open source

On the receipt of any information in an investigation, it is likely that a given amount of open source research will be required. To do this, authorisation may be required (see Chapter 4 in relation to surveillance on the Internet).

Before embarking online, due attention and consideration must be given to the following.

- Is it possible that your online activity will leave digital footprints?

- Is there a need to perform these online enquiries?

- Has the appropriate risk assessment been made?

- Has the appropriate level of surveillance authority been obtained?

- Are the actions such that authority is required for the investigator to be registered as a covert human intelligence source (CHIS)?

- The mere fact that information is publicly available does not preclude it from being private information.

Using search engines

When an investigator enters a keyword or phrase into a search engine, the engine examines its index and provides a listing of best-matching web pages, usually with a short synopsis containing the document's title and parts of the text. The majority of search engines support the use of the *Boolean operators* AND, OR and NOT to further specify the search query. Some search engines provide an advanced feature called 'proximity search', which allows investigators to define the distance between keywords.

The quality of a search engine depends on the significance of the set of results it returns. While there may be hundreds of web pages that include a particular keyword or phrase, some may be more pertinent, popular or trustworthy than others. Most search engines employ methods to grade the results to provide the so-called 'best' results first. How a search engine decides which pages are the best, and what order they should be shown in, varies widely from one engine to another. As new technologies emerge and our use of the Internet changes, so do the methods used by search engines.

The majority of web-based search engines are commercial enterprises supported by advertising takings and, as a result, some allow advertisers to pay money to have their listings ranked higher in search results. Those search engines that do not accept money for their search results, make money by running search-related adverts along with the regular search results. Money is generated every time a user clicks on one of these adverts.

The invisible web

Search engines crawl the web looking for new web pages. To do this they use *web crawlers*, also known as web spiders and robots. These crawlers read the web pages and put the information gained into a large database or index that the public can access and search. None of them covers the entire net, but some are rather large.

There is a problem here that most people online are not conscious of: there are vast areas of the web that are completely invisible to the search engines. Some believe that the 'invisible web', also known as the 'deep web', is increasing faster than the visible web that most people are familiar with. This part of the web consists of information that is held on specialised databases and, unlike web pages on the visible net, the information in these databases is generally inaccessible to the software crawlers that bring together search engine indexes.

Metasearch engines

This type of search engine is one that sends user requests to a number of other search engines and/or databases and aggregates the results into a list according to where they originate. They enable investigators to access several search engines simultaneously with one or more search terms. They function on the principle that the Internet and the web are too large for any one search engine to index it all, and that more wide-ranging search results can be achieved by combining the results from several search engines. This also may save the investigator from having to use multiple search engines separately.

Web pages and websites

HTML web pages can be removed instantly from a server, which can be a problem when an investigator is trying to prove the existence of a given page. However, there are websites, such as *Wayback Machine*, that can prove useful in retrieving old or unavailable web pages. These groups of electronic files are stored on computers located all over the world. The Internet is known as a client-server system, and large websites can often use multiple servers.

You access a website by typing in the URL and, through the use of a DNS and routers, the website sought sends data to you over the Internet. Your web browser software, such as Microsoft IE or Netscape Navigator, interprets the data and displays it on the computer screen. When your browser receives web data, it knows what to do with it because it is written in the computer language HTML.

One of the properties of HTML that has made the web so popular is its universal programming language; this ensures that it can run on any computer operating system, from DOS to Windows. Using just an HTML page, an investigator can work backwards to prove that the user asked for a file and that it was not given to them.

A website has one or more pages that usually relate to a common theme, such as a business, person, organisation or subject. The first page is called the home page, which acts as an index, indicating the content of the site. From the home page, the user can click on hyperlinks to access other web pages, therefore repeating the data-flow process.

PRACTICAL TASK

Access the following websites, and look for specialised and reference search engines. Then select a subject matter and see how the results from each can vary.

- *www.lib.berkeley.edu/TeachingLib/Guides/Internet/InvisibleWeb.html http://en.wikipedia. org/wiki/Deep_Web*

- *www.archive.org/index.php*

- *http://en.wikipedia.org/wiki/Domain_name_system*

- *www.lib.berkeley.edu/TeachingLib/Guides/Internet/FindInfo.html*

- *www.searchingtheinternet.info/*

Email

Investigators need to be aware that Internet users like HTML email as it gives them the capability to animate the mail by using diverse colours, font sizes and styles, plus the opportunity to introduce pictures and sounds. It is also opportune that the original design for HTML has a very open and tolerant set of rules, so if, for example, a browser encounters a footnote it does not know how to deal with or display, it simply ignores it.

Web-based email

The most common web-based email programs are Hotmail and Yahoo, which create slightly different versions of HTML pages. These common programs use names such as 'Compose', 'Get' or the title of the page. Due to them not handling their cache files in the same way, in order to analyse them an investigator should attempt to locate items that are not based on file names, but rather data contained within the cache file, consistent with the type of web mail being examined. In computer science a *cache*, pronounced 'cash', is a temporary storage area where frequently accessed data can be copied and stored for easier and faster access.

For intelligence purposes, once these files are identified they can be forensically recovered and viewed using a third-party HTML viewer. The information required can be found in:

- cache files;
- temporary Internet files;
- unallocated disc space;
- swap files;
- hibernate files.

Examination of URLs and the cache files can reveal how a user accesses the cache in IE and the URLs visited by their web browser. Further examination of this cache can also reveal email-addressed files.

The opening and viewing of these files may only show the contents of received mail. This is because some web-based email gives the user an option to prevent email being stored in the browser's cache.

Email analysis

Information from the content of an email is self-explanatory, as is the content of any attached material; however, additional information can be found in the header information. By selecting an email message and right clicking, 'Properties' can be selected and the 'Details' tab will supply the header information.

There are clues in an email that indicate where the email originated. All computers have a unique address that is stored in a section of the email called a *header*. Just as a letter travels through several post offices before arriving in a letterbox, an email travels through several servers before arriving in a computer inbox. Each server leaves a mark by inserting its address in the header of an email and so reveals the path that the message has taken from the sender to the recipient.

However, it should be noted that someone with sufficient technical knowledge would be able to 'spoof' an email header quite easily. What a person actually does is to alter the data within the header, therefore hiding their identity by the insertion of false information.

The most important header attribute for tracing purposes is the received header (RH) field. Every time an email moves through a new mail server, a new RH line is added to the beginning of the header's list. This means that, as you read the RH from top to bottom, you are gradually moving closer to the computer/person that sent the email.

As previously stated, a four-part number like 233.16.10.73 is known as an IP address. IP stands for *Internet Protocol*, which is a standard used by all machines on the Internet in order to communicate. For a computer to do any Internet-related task, it needs an IP address and your ISP assigns these every time you connect to the Internet. Some ISPs provide you with a static IP address, which never changes each time you connect to the Internet, but most ISPs provide dynamic IP addresses that do change every time you connect.

The criminal fraternity regularly uses email communications to commit illegal activities, such as fraud and phishing scams, as well as for transmitting threats and viruses. However, it can be avoided if you keep your email address as secret as possible, ignore unsolicited emails by deleting them and realising that, if it looks too good to be true, then it is.

Time analysis

Every time you receive an email, the information is sent behind the scenes to your unique IP address. To avoid conflicts, no two computers can have the same IP address, as this would cause confusion as to which computer should receive the information. Subsequently, by providing the IP address and full email Internet headers (containing time-of-day information) to the sender's ISP, the unique end-user can be tracked down by examining login and logout information.

PRACTICAL TASK

Go to an email that you have received, right click on the email and select 'Properties' from the drop-down box, and then click on the 'Details' tab. This will then present you with the route the email has taken from the sender to you.

Then go to www.emailaddressmanager.com/tips/header.html and use the information provided to analyse the content of your 'Details'.

Sources of intelligence

Here, there should be a holistic approach – not only should the investigator use open source and email intelligence, but he or she should also consider the following additional sources of digital intelligence:

- forensic analysis of internal and external computer media, including historical analysis;
- proactive covert Internet operations;
- online covert human intelligence sources (CHIS).

A recent good example of open source analysis was when a bounty hunter identified a drug dealer from his MySpace and Facebook profiles. The drug dealer had been facing 15 years in prison, but jumped bail in Florida, USA, and went to Surrey, England; to help him stay hidden, he changed his name by deed poll. Unluckily for the drug dealer, he set up profiles on MySpace and Facebook using his new name but with his own photograph. The bounty hunter was able to find him by following a new link that had appeared on the profiles of the drug dealer's friends.

This type of online investigative work, and the increase in computer crime, have resulted in the need for specific guidelines for the investigation and collection of intelligence and evidence. In response, ACPO has issued guidelines in the UK, which are in turn used as a template for similar guidelines by other international law enforcement agencies.

PRACTICAL TASK

Access the ACPO report – Good Practice Guide for Computer-Based Electronic Evidence *(www.7safe.com/electronic_evidence/#) and find the four key principles of computer-based evidence on page 6. Get to know the four principles and read through the explanation of them. Write down what you consider to be the key messages here for a cyber-crime investigator.*

Internet investigative strategies

The investigation of an Internet crime has three primary objectives:

- to locate the computer connected to the Internet that is the source of the suspect activity;
- to identify and locate the person using the computer when the activity occurred;
- to find and secure digital intelligence.

Using the Internet to build up intelligence requires stricter standards of proof and it requires a degree of caution on the part of the investigator. However, using network and Internet investigative techniques will assist an investigator in attempting to identify computers. This transparent connectivity is the basis for how the Internet works; however, with some effort a user can travel the Internet and the web without leaving traces.

Finding the computer

Tracing an email is probably the most common way to find a person on the Internet. At the same time, hiding the authorship of an email or the computer it was sent from is probably the most common way people hide their identity on the Internet. Most do it for reasons of privacy, but some take advantage of this ability to help them commit crimes. People who want to surf the web with some privacy often use *anonymous remailers*. An anonymous remailer is a service or software that removes header information from email and often sends it through several different servers to disguise its origin. They are easy for even the inexperienced to use and can be very effective in hiding the sender of a message. In the near future, computing power and investigative ingenuity may provide the opportunity to trace back to the source.

Information distribution

The majority of sites on the web contain commercial content, a small percentage contain scientific or educational content, and an even lower percentage contain pornographic content. Search engines are more likely to index commercial sites than any other, and no engine is capable of indexing the entire web; in fact, it has been acknowledged that some leading search engines can take weeks to index a new website.

To prove the definite existence of a web page, a clear and precise understanding of where information can be found on the Internet is required, and an investigator must always consider permanence, authenticity and origin.

- **Permanence**: Can the data be deleted? Is it likely to be deleted?

- **Authenticity**: This is the accurate provenance of origin, such as the authorship of an email message or a Word document.

- **Origin**: Where and when was the data created? Who created it?

Newsgroups

Newsgroups are much like the public message boards on old bulletin board systems. For those readers not familiar with this idea, picture an electronic version of the corkboard at a school or university. They regularly become cliquish and are subject to periodic flaming and trolling (see the next task for an explanation), but they can also be a priceless source of information. They bring people who are interested in specific topics of interest together from around the globe.

How do they work?

Classically, a newsgroup is fixed on a particular subject. Some newsgroups permit the posting of messages and articles on a wide assortment of themes. The administrator will decide on how long articles are kept on the server before being deleted. Different servers will have different retention times for the same newsgroup – some may keep articles for as little as one or two weeks, while others may retain them for many months.

Newsgroups are a useful source of intelligence, but in order to access them an investigator will require a newsreader program. There are also search engines that let you search newsgroups and the archives of newsgroups.

PRACTICAL TASK

- Go to *www.bbc.co.uk/dna/h2g2/A1082512* and find out what the terms 'flaming' and 'trolling' mean. Then find out why people feel the need to behave in this manner and how an individual should respond to it.

- If you have never seen a newsgroup on the Internet, go to *http://groups.google.co.uk* and find out how to set up and access a newsgroup, and explore some of the content of already established newsgroups.

C H A P T E R   S U M M A R Y

There has been an increase in the level of e-crime within the UK and globally. Online criminality continues to take advantage of the opportunities created by the worldwide increase in computer networks. The quotation below eloquently provides a graphic view of the extent of the problem:

> Although cyber investigation is still in the early stages of its development, the burgeoning use of the internet has increased the necessity for digital investigations. If the police and other authorities do not stay on top of this problem, they may lose the battle to control this cyber-crime explosion.
>
> (Kao and Wang, 2009, p207)

In this chapter you have been provided with information on a blend of publicly available and accessible materials on the Internet, also known as unclassified or competitive intelligence. Technical processes must be combined with investigators' skill to produce Internet information and intelligence reports that are specific to a subject, an event or an individual. All this can be used to harmonise information, intelligence or evidence obtained by other means; it should not be a replacement for them.

The investigator's challenge is to dig out the maximum amount of digital intelligence from the examination of stored data or digital artefacts, and in order to achieve this the investigator needs an understanding of the environment that housed it and a sound knowledge of computer crime.

Kao, Da-Yu and Wang, Shiu-Jeng (2009) The IP address and time in Cyber crime investigation. *Policing: An International Journal of Strategies & Management*, 32(2): 194–208.

Cyber-crime prevention

www.banksafeonline.org.uk (Bank Safe Online)

www.besafeonline.org (Be Safe Online)

www.scambusters.org (Scam Busters)

www.staysafeonline.info (Stay Safe Online)

Child protection

www.ceop.gov.uk (Child Exploitation and Online Protection Centre)

www.cyberangels.org (CyberAngels – a program of Guardian Angels)

www.iwf.org.uk (Internet Watch Foundation)

www.virtualglobaltaskforce.com (Virtual Global Taskforce)

Law enforcement agencies

www.fraud.org/welcome.htm (US National Fraud Information Center)

www.homeoffice.gov.uk/inside/org/dob/direct/ntac.html (National Technical Assistance Centre)

www.interpol.int/Public/TechnologyCrime/default.asp (Interpol – Information Technology Crime)

www.justice.gov/criminal/cybercrime (Computer Crime & Intellectual Property Section, US Department of Justice)

www.nw3c.org (National White Collar Crime Centre)

Computer Misuse Act 1990

Criminal Procedure and Investigations Act 1996

Human Rights Act 1998

Data Protection Act 1998

Data Retention (EC Directive) Regulations 2009

Freedom of Information Act 2000

Regulation of Investigatory Powers Act 2000

3 Investigation of cyber-crime

CHAPTER OBJECTIVES

By the end of this chapter you should be able to:

- understand of some of the processes, procedures and problems that an investigator can come across when investigating a cyber-crime;
- develop a skill base in relation to the abuse and criminal use of IT;
- give an overview of the legal, ethical and professional standards that must be taken into consideration;
- explain some of the issues in relation to the evidence that is sought in investigations of cyber-crime.

LINKS TO STANDARDS

This chapter provides opportunities for links with the following Skills for Justice, National Occupational Standards (NOS) for Policing and Law Enforcement 2008.

CO1   Identify and secure electronic evidence sources.
CO3   Capture and preserve electronic evidence.
CO4   Investigate electronic evidence.
CO5   Evaluate and report electronic evidence.

Introduction

Cyber-crime has become part of everyday business for organised crime (Verizon Business, 2009, p2) and the profile of your typical cyber-criminal is changing rapidly, from an insignificant student who is ridiculed as being affected or boringly studious, to a member of the upper echelon of the criminal fraternity, which is by tradition associated with armed robbery, drug supply, people trafficking and money laundering.

In general, it is accepted that 'cyber-crime' means any crime committed using a computer or a computer network, and this type of crime has generated a new cyberworld, complete with its own communities, languages and cultures. However, let's not get carried away by the mystique of these new and emerging technologies – cyber-crime is, in the main, the criminal use of 'new tools' for 'old crimes'.

It is also not restricted to criminal prosecutions; there are other incidences, such as employment disputes, security breaches and the theft of intellectual property. It can also be described as 'computer abuse', but whatever you call it, if not handled properly it can and does cause considerable problems.

On a global scale, cyber-crime is progressing at an exceptional rate as a result of the advancement of the electronic medium. While advancements are being made in combating cyber-crime, a void continues to exist in legislative compatibility across jurisdictions. On a regular basis, the headlines of national newspapers carry news of the latest cyber-crime that has been discovered, including that involving major corporations whose computers have been hacked.

But what people in general do not realise is that cyber-crime is becoming even more sophisticated. In the same way that all of us use computers increasingly in our businesses and personal lives, so too are criminals using computers, not just to commit high-tech offences, but to plan, research and coordinate a wide variety of crimes – what we now call cyber-crimes.

The part computers play in crime and, in particular, the uncovering and prosecution of crime has never been as noteworthy as it is today; for example, the attempted fraud against the Sumitomo Mitsui Bank in the City of London in September 2006.

CASE STUDY

The security of Sumitomo Mitsui Bank premises was contracted to a buildings security firm, and their staff had out-of-hours access to the bank's offices, in which computers that were used for processing transactions using the Swift (Society for Worldwide Financial Telecommunication) system were kept. Swift is a protected system for the transfer of funds electronically between banks.

The head of the contracted security team provided unauthorised physical access to bank premises for two males outside normal working hours and over a weekend period. The two intruders were technically knowledgeable and attempted to transfer considerable funds to foreign bank accounts, using the said Swift payments system.

This attempt used commercial keystroke-logging software installed in computers that were used to process Swift transactions. Over a period of time, the key loggers facilitated the collection of user IDs and passwords.

Then, over a weekend period, these stolen login credentials were used in an attempt to transfer £229 million to multiple overseas accounts, which were under the control of fraudsters. However, due to the authentication process in the Swift system, it rejected the transfers and no financial losses were incurred.

The premises' external CCTV camera settings had been adjusted in an attempt to obscure the entry and exit of the intruders. Also, in an attempt to slow down the discovery of the illegal activity, the intruders carried out a disk format on all computers in the office. In addition, docking stations (to which laptops can be connected) had their cables cut. This was aimed at temporarily preventing staff from accessing the Swift system on the following Monday morning.

When the investigation in the UK concluded, three defendants pleaded guilty and two were found guilty after a trial.

One of the key participants was 'Lord' Hugh Rodley. He was described as the 'chief executive' of this criminal enterprise. At the time, it was said that he owed money to a number of criminals within the UK criminal fraternity and he himself had a criminal history dating back some 30 years. He also lived in a £2 million mansion in Tewkesbury. On 5 March 2009, Rodley was sentenced to eight years' imprisonment for his part in what is reported as the UK's biggest ever cyber-crime case.

What you should take particular note of as a result of the case described above are:

- the dangers that key loggers pose;
- the need to implement cyber-crime prevention measures in relation to third parties;
- the international cooperation between French, Belgian and British law enforcement;
- how overlapping pieces of evidence, from both traditional and electronic evidence, can be effectively used in a prosecution.

For the case described above, access the following and other online resources for further information.

- *www.theregister.co.uk/2009/03/19/sumitomo_cyberheist_investigation/page3.html*
- *http://news.bbc.co.uk/1/hi/uk/7909595.stm*
- *www.guardian.co.uk/uk/2009/mar/05/lord-of-fraud-bank-raid*

Read the reports, make a list of the investigative measures that were used, and consider how they contributed to the successful prosecution of 'Lord' Hugh Rodley and others.

Cyber-crime

Information communication and Internet technology are evolving at a tremendous pace, and while this is providing vast opportunities for legitimate users, it is also giving criminals similar opportunities.

The global cost of cyber-crime is currently estimated to be one trillion dollars a year (Mills, 2009), and this type of crime has no regional, national or international boundaries. This is unlike law enforcement, which has physical and remit boundaries and limits in relation to jurisdiction. This all contributes to making cyber-crime an intriguing area of crime investigation.

As organisations become more digitally complex and exchange more data online, cyber-crime will increase and at a rapid pace. Therefore, the responsibility must be on law enforcement and the private sector to establish best practice in relation to cyber-crime, and serious consideration needs to be given to how confidential and sensitive information can be efficiently and effectively exchanged. It is apparent that most cyber-crime is not detected and is difficult to scope; therefore, it is a growing global problem.

Those who commit unlawful and illegal actions using a computer exploit weaknesses in systems, and these actions are frequently facilitated by poor security procedures and a lack of intelligence analysis. This also means that the skills of the cyber-crime investigator must constantly evolve in order to keep pace with new software and devices that can store electronic data.

Defining and combating cyber-crime

Since 2001, progress has been made in relation to global actions to define and combat cyber-crime (CoE, 2001); however, there is still a large gap that exists in legislative compatibility across international borders. At that time, the Council of Europe aimed to harmonise definitions of cyber-crime and procedures for warrants and evidence collection across international jurisdictions. In addition, it aimed to provide significant guidance on evidential standards.

The CoE *Convention on Cybercrime* was signed on 23 November 2001 and the resultant legislation was the first piece of international legislation covering the criminal use of information technology. Although the CoE is a regional body, the *Convention* provides for a global framework for law enforcement in cyberspace; non-member states of the CoE, such as Canada, Japan and the USA, contributed to its preparation. The *Convention on Cybercrime* (CoE, 2001) came into being on 1 July 2004 and produced the following principles.

- When dealing with digital evidence, all of the general forensic and procedural principles must be applied.

- Upon seizing digital evidence, actions taken should not change that evidence.

- When it is necessary for a person to access original digital evidence, that person should be trained for the purpose.

- All activity relating to the seizure, access, storage or transfer of digital evidence must be fully documented, preserved and available for review.

- An individual is responsible for all actions taken with respect to digital evidence while that evidence is in their possession.

- Any agency that is responsible for seizing, accessing, storing or transferring digital evidence, is responsible for compliance with these principles.

REFLECTIVE TASK

Go to http://conventions.coe.int/Treaty/en/Treaties/html/185.htm to find the CoE's Convention on Cybercrime, read through the report and consider the supporting information it provides for establishing the principles above. Analyse the content and decide if you believe that the report is still valid today or whether it needs updating.

This task should be repeated once you have completed all of the tasks in this chapter.

Cyber-crime: the problems

Cyber-crime, hi-tech crime, e-crime, or whatever you choose to call it, has no boundaries, particularly in relation to jurisdiction. We have no *corpus juris*; in other words, countries all have different legal systems. More than any other global crime, the swiftness and flexibility of cyber-crime challenges existing regulation and legislation. It can and is perpetrated from anywhere in the world against any computer.

Added to that problem is something that is often overlooked – the profiling of cyber-crime and the cyber-criminal. The idea that an individual committing crime in cyberspace can fit a certain profile may seem far-fetched, but evidence suggests that certain distinguishing characteristics do regularly exist in the most common types of cyber-criminals. This can be particularly useful for investigative bodies and organisations that are attempting to do away with cyber-criminals inside their own walls (Verizon Business, 2009).

The insider is a very real problem and some organisations spend a lot of money on an annual basis in an attempt to detect any such action before it happens. A good example of this is the Sumitomo Mitsui Bank (see Case study on pages 35–6), which now has staff using one-time passwords and fingerprint checks to log on to any of the bank's systems (Young, 2009).

Another complex problem involves security breaches, because when one takes place the amount of data compromised is not always known. Also, when missing data is retrieved, if the data is not protected – that is, encrypted – there is no assurance that it has not already been duplicated, stored elsewhere, or forwarded to another. The problem is further complicated by the fact that some organisations fail to recognise that they are losing data, because they do not know that they have that data in the first place. This high level of data loss ensures that offenders have an abundant supply of new marketable data.

But, as with every other economy, if you're going to flood the market with goods, what will happen to the price? With more and more stolen records flooding the underground market, the cost of one stolen record has dropped. That means that, from a cyber-criminal's perspective, if you still want to make some money, you have to steal a lot more data or data that is much more valuable. This is further complicated by the fact that almost 70 per cent of all victims of a data breach have to find out that they have lost their data through a third party (Verizon Business, 2009, p3) and, in addition, in 2009, 70 per cent of households in the UK had Internet access. All this makes the potential number of victims for the cyber-criminal to attack much greater (National Statistics, 2009).

Finally, the social and economic impacts of cyber-crime are progressively growing and, as evidenced by the surveys researched, they are anticipated to increase even further in the future. This type of crime strikes at two main areas: first, the growth and development of a country's economy; and, second, the transformation of a country into an information society. This was identified and evidenced a few years ago by a report from the European Society Group and the Institute for Public Policy Research, who stated: 'the cost to industry and individuals of electronically assisted crime may have already far outstretched that of physical crime' (EURIM/IPPR, 2005). This statement is still very valid today and means that there certainly is a major problem with cyber-crime and we need a thorough understanding of the problem so as to be able to investigate it professionally.

Types of cyber-crime

We have already identified that cyber-crime has become a rapidly growing phenomenon over recent years. Computers, and in particular the Internet, provide great benefits for society. However, the real threat is that criminals are exploiting these media, turning tools designed to benefit society into tools to help them commit a variety of crimes.

First, there are 'new crimes, new tools' – new opportunities for crimes against computers and IT networks that present new challenges to law enforcement agencies, for example hacking and viruses, denial of service attacks, and spoof websites.

The second type of cyber-crime, as mentioned earlier, is 'new tools, old crimes' – traditional crimes supported by the use of the Internet and hi-technology, such as fraud, blackmail and extortion, paedophilia, pornography, identity theft and cyber-stalking.

These offences can be put into one or more of the following categories of cyber-crime, but note that this is not a comprehensive list.

- **Pornography**: Computers are used to store and distribute pornographic images, both still and moving.
- **Theft and fraud**: Computers and network systems are used to divert and steal money or property.
- **Internet auctions**: After sending your money, you may receive nothing at all or an item that is less valuable than promised.
- **Internet access services**: You may be 'trapped' into a long-term contract for Internet access, with big penalties for early cancellation.
- **Web cramming**: You receive an invoice or charge on your telephone bill for services you haven't agreed to.

- **Multi-level marketing (MLM) and pyramid scams**: You buy into an MLM plan primarily for enrolling other people into the scheme, often without any product or service being delivered. Other examples include advanced fee frauds, 'pump and dump' share pushing and a host of other 'get rich quick' schemes.

- **Credit card fraud**: Fraudulent promoters ask for your credit card number for age verification or some other supposedly legitimate reason, and then run up charges on your card.

- **Obfuscated URLs, phishing and enterprise phishing attacks**: These involve rogue emails, usually purporting to be from legitimate financial institutions.

- **Denial of service (DOS) attacks**: Also known as distributed denial of service (DDOS) attacks, these occur when hackers cause damage or corruption to an ISP's systems and databases. Networks are paralysed and are rendered unusable. This type of attack can be accompanied with or without threats.

- **Web sabotage**: This is where hackers access legitimate websites and either alter their appearance and change information, or set up a replica site with false or misleading information.

- **Email-related offences**: These include cyber-stalking, obscenity emailing, death threats and many more.

- **Account hacking**: A genuine Internet account is used without the knowledge of the account holder, either by hacking with software or by using an account where the genuine user's access details have been compromised. There is currently a noteworthy shift towards this type of offence. It does involve the offender having the ability to access a victim's bank, mail or social networking accounts with the intention of committing or facilitating an unlawful act, such as fraud. There is a distinct move in criminal methods of operation, from opening new accounts with stolen identities to accessing existing accounts.

PRACTICAL TASK

Find the US Department of Justice, Computer Crime & Intellectual Property Section, which is at www.justice.gov/criminal/cybercrime, and identify real-life examples of cyber-crime as defined above. The investigations will emphasise the information that you will become familiar with as you advance through this book.

In addition, and in order to expand your knowledge of the various cyber-crimes, identify any cyber-crime offences that are not listed above.

Cyber-crime motives

Understanding the reasons why certain types of crime are committed and the motivations of criminals helps in the initial stages of a cyber-crime investigation, as an investigator may then be better able to understand the digital clues that are left behind by the offender.

For example, once confidential or sensitive information has been obtained through a security breach, the offenders are going to want to use it or sell it, or it can soon lose its value once the breach has been discovered, either by the victim or by the illegal use of other data that were stolen at the same time.

Many cyber offenders do not want to get caught and do not want to make their activities known in online social networking websites. In contrast, some offenders do need to boast about their exploits, as their purpose is to gain notoriety among the online community.

The following list shows that the possibility of detection of a cyber-crime, and of the identification of the offender, is associated with motive; although numerous motives are possible, one may prevail over the others. Familiar motives for cyber-crimes include:

- ideological and/or political reasons;
- retaliation or reprisal;
- notoriety or celebrity status;
- industrial espionage and competitive advantage;
- obtaining goods, money or services by deception;
- hiding evidence of a crime;
- financial gain through such crimes as blackmail.

Following on from motives, we have the modes of attack. These can be put into three categories and are defined by how the attack takes place.

- **Insider attacks**: These involve a breach of trust from an employee, management, consultants, or temporary staff from within an organisation.
- **External attacks**: These involve hackers hired by an insider, a competitor or even a former employee, whose aim is to steal monies, proprietary software, confidential information or personal identities, or to destroy an organisation's reputation.
- **Blended attacks**: These are external or internal attacks that occur because of an unintentional act or a premeditated action by an insider or a third party.

The target of cyber-crime can either be a target of choice, where the attack is directed or focused at a particular individual or organisation, or a target of opportunity, where the attack is random or autonomous. To be factored with this is the probability of detection; that is, is it a stealth attack, where the offender wants to avoid detection, or a highly visible and blatant attack, where the offender wants to be noticed or detected?

Steps in an investigation

First, you should note that, at the commencement of any investigation, the investigator(s) will never know what they may come across, and only too often they find more than they could have imagined.

In any investigation, the investigator must follow a particular process. This starts with analysing the complaint, asking questions and documenting the results, in order that the crime can be identified, as well as the venue where it took place and the location of the evidence.

However, are investigators ready to handle cyber-crime evidence? In other words, do they have in place the basic steps to conduct such an investigation, and in what format should the investigation be conducted? In generic terms, there is a systematic approach to the examination process and to cyber-crime work.

1. Analysis of the complaint.

2. Acceptance and prioritisation of the investigation.

3. Case assessment, including the appropriate authority to seize evidence.

4. Collecting physical evidence.

5. Forensic evidential acquisition.

6. Forensic and 'real-world' evidential examination.

7. Interviewing witnesses and suspects.

8. Intelligence analysis.

9. Analysis of the case.

10. Conducting follow-up lines of enquiry, if required.

11. Producing a report and/or statement, along with exhibits.

12. Reviewing the case and deciding whether to prosecute.

Investigators should, wherever possible, follow the same or similar generic process each time they conduct an investigation. This will go towards ensuring that they do not miss, or fail to complete, significant tasks. Their actions and the results of those actions need to be documented.

An investigator also needs to be aware that, in any such investigation, the electronic media will fall into one or more of the following four categories.

- The computer is the crime instrument.

- The computer is incidental to a traditional crime.

- The computer facilitates a crime.

- It is a new crime generated by the prevalence of the computer.

Investigative obstacles

Various obstacles do stand in the way of successfully prosecuting cyber-criminals, which include the difficulty of defining the crime in the first instance, and the jurisdictional problems that arise when the victim(s) and offender(s) are in different geographic locations. With regard to jurisdiction, investigators must be ready for legal difficulties when cyber-crimes cross national and international boundaries.

This is further complicated by the attitude and lifestyle differences that exist both nationally and globally. However, it is possible to overcome all these challenges and put together a case that will stand up in court, for example the Sumitomo Mitsui Bank investigation (see pages 35–6). This investigation proves that, globally, investigators can work with prosecutors to make sure that they recognise the elements that must be proven to identify, arrest and convict in a cyber-crime investigation.

Private-sector professional personnel, who foresee themselves working with law enforcement on cyber-crime investigations, can gain knowledge of how national and international criminal justice systems operate, and can learn to recognise the differences between regulatory and criminal laws, and which specific elements fall under which investigative bodies of law in their jurisdiction.

Investigative process

The basic investigative process is to identify the offender and the methodology involved, including the vulnerability of the computer and/or network that allowed the offender to gain access to the system. The evidence must then be preserved for any civil or criminal proceedings.

This means that cyber-crime investigators must be familiar with the process of gathering digital data and other information and intelligence that might be related to the commission of an offence, which is, in fact, the definition of a criminal investigation.

IT and other security professionals who work with law enforcement to smooth the progress of a case might be intimidated by the word 'investigation' and its official implications, but it is easier to comprehend if you recognise that we all perform investigations all the time. Every time we meet a new person, make a major purchase, or make a major life decision, such as changing jobs, we investigate. The process is simply the gathering of information. A network administrator often has reasons to investigate, such as when a server crashes or when a user is unable to access his or her profile, etc.

The differences between these two types of investigation lie in their aims and objectives. In both instances, the key objective is to gather information. In a criminal investigation, that information is eventually used to prove the guilt or the innocence of an accused person. Thus, the process must be formalised to make available a model structure that ensures conformity with the laws that govern evidence collection.

Nevertheless, it is vital for investigators to keep in mind that even evidence that is not admissible in formal proceedings can still be valuable during the course of the investigation, because it can help the investigator view the circumstances of the unlawful act and can help him or her seek other ways to make that evidence admissible and/or to find new evidence.

For presentation in any proceedings, evidence must be evaluated using one or all of the following questions.

- Is it relevant?
- Is it material?

- Is it competent?

- Is it believable?

- Is the witness credible?

- Has the evidence been tampered with?

The purpose of any investigation is to establish the truth and cyber-crime is no different in this respect. Investigators should put away personal opinion and approach the investigation with an open mind, adopting the 5WH questioning method: to find out who, what, when, where, why and how.

Investigative difficulties

The main way to improve cyber-security is to reduce the number of compromised systems and the amount of time that a system stays in a compromised state. The reality is that few attacks are launched directly from cyber-criminals' systems, since they know they would be easily caught using standard backtracking methods.

Such an investigative strategy can be complicated; for example, once a computer has been attacked, backtracking of the modus operandi will reveal an IP address. However, like tracking telephone numbers, this will not necessarily give you the offender's identity, which under normal circumstances would mean the investigative trail would stop. Investigators then have to rely on other lines of enquiry, such as the 'money trail', similar offences, CHIS or arrests/intelligence from other law enforcement and financial institutions. All of this is very time-consuming and the final outcome will not necessarily produce a satisfactory result.

Then there are other general investigative difficulties; for example, any evidence found in a cyber-crime investigation may implicate a computer, but you still need to tie a person to that computer – the person whose fingers were on the keyboard.

Objectives of computer forensics

We know that the aim of a cyber-crime investigator is to establish the nature and events concerning a crime and to trace the offender by following a well thought-out investigative procedure. This can be aided by the forensic examination of digital evidence after an incident has taken place. Here, investigators must apply the following two tests to that evidence, so that it can be accepted into any formal proceedings: first, authenticity – the correct attribution of origin; and, second, reliability – is the evidence steadfast, true and right?

The actual forensic analysis should only take place on an image of the original evidence. The investigator needs to be able to show a third party that it was a thorough examination and that the evidence is authentic and unaltered. The last part is usually achieved by the use of algorithms for verification, also known as 'hash' values (see Chapter 5 for more detail on forensic evidence).

Evidence

The first forensic laboratory was set up in 1920 by Doctor Edmund Locard to study how to use trace or contact evidence to solve crimes. His theory was that, during a crime, there was an exchange of physical evidence between the offender and the crime scene. He put forward a theory called the exchange principle (Chisum and Turvey, 2000), which states that, whenever an offender comes into contact with a victim or an object, or is present at a crime scene, he or she will leave behind some evidence and also take away some evidence. For example, a car thief will leave traces of being there, such as fingerprints, and take traces away with them, such as seat fibres. Crimes committed using or against a computer also leave trace evidence.

Therefore, after identifying the suspect(s) and any sources of evidence, investigators must know where to find such evidence, and must preserve it, analyse it and maintain its continuity, and only then will they be able to present their findings.

Where to find the evidence

Every cyber-crime has certain distinctive aspects, and these determine the steps that are taken to produce digital evidence or intelligence, and often it comes down to knowing where and what to look for. Take, for example, the case of Doctor Harold Shipman. He was a medical doctor who was one of the most prolific serial killers in the UK and the world. He was responsible for at least 236 murders between 1975 and 1998 (Dodd, 2001), and was suspected of many more. The forensic analysis of his computer showed investigators that he had changed medical records and this was a significant piece of evidence that contributed to his conviction.

Disclosure

This is the process that forms part of legal proceedings, whereby parties inform other parties of the existence of any relevant evidence that is, or has been, in their control (the legislation, the Criminal Procedure and Investigations Act 1996, is discussed in more detail in next chapter). This compares with the civil process known as 'discovery' and focuses on the existence of any relevant documents that are, or have been, in the parties' control.

This is a major area of concern for all investigations in which the recovery of electronic evidence is necessary. The increasing size of computer storage media is making the examination of all the contents a daunting task. At present, a series of predetermined checks and procedures is adopted in an effort to satisfy disclosure requirements. Wherever possible, digital searches have to be targeted, and to date there have been no problems with the practices adopted. However, prosecutors and defence alike are not necessarily aware of the volume of data held on computers, and as a result they do not always ask the right questions, or they sometimes impose unrealistic demands or timescales.

There are also cases where inextricably linked material exists on the same media and, due to the large volume or fragmentary nature of the data, viewing all of it may be impossible, or may require a disproportionate use of resources. There are also instances where automatic disclosure cannot be permitted, for example in the case of a malicious code, the return of which to a suspect could result in further criminal acts.

There can also be problems in cross-disclosure cases that involve multiple defendants, or in cases involving legally privileged material, or personal data relating to persons not under suspicion, or who may become at risk if disclosure is made to other suspects. There may be commercially sensitive data contained within the material. Also, in the case of, for example, CCTV images, where the collection of data is indiscriminate, consideration should be given to the collateral intrusion into the privacy of others.

Those who embrace the implementation of disclosure best practices will benefit from the reward it offers. Incredibly few businesses have the management structures in place to allow them to carry out an efficient and cost-effective forensic investigation, and, as a consequence, obtain disclosure. This becomes more poignant when an organisation is drawn into an investigation against its will. In criminal and civil proceedings, the other party, or a party entitled to do so, is at liberty to require disclosure or discovery of data from a computer system.

Corporations versus law enforcement

The private sector does not have the physical, organisational and jurisdictional responsibilities of law enforcement. However, the expectation of reputational damage should be a major incentive for the likes of financial institutions to ensure that their computer networks are free from internal and external abuse and are protected against cyber-crime. Therefore, would it not be wise for them to invest time and effort in making computer systems secure and working closely with law enforcement? Yes, it would, but it would require a financial commitment, which many are not prepared to take on. However, the alternative could be onerous, not just in terms of direct costs, but also in terms of collateral intrusion and the resultant legal claims of third parties.

When engaged in stopping cyber-crime, some organisations do focus on minimising reputational damage and financial damage by controlling the results of unauthorised access attempts, and by the prevention, detection and, if possible, identification of unauthorised actions and computer abuse. The financial damage occurs when it becomes public knowledge that the organisation has been subjected to a cyber-crime, which will harm investor confidence and frighten away current and potential customers. What corporations also fear is the effect of having confidential and sensitive data seized by law enforcement. As a consequence, most organisations perceive that there is little advantage in reporting cyber-crimes to law enforcement.

Whereas the priorities for law enforcement are prosecution, disruption and dismantlement, as has been discussed previously in this and other chapters, for cases to be prosecuted, evidence must be properly collected, processed and preserved. However, once the web is involved, crimes can be committed across borders, thereby involving a number of jurisdictional issues.

Cyber-crime prevention

The main priority for all must be to concentrate on prevention, taking steps to provide security for data and systems, rather than on detecting crimes once they have been committed. It is this proactive approach that can make a real difference.

To do this we first have to recognise that there are similarities between cyber-crime security and traditional crime prevention. If an organisation's physical precautions are strong, criminals will look elsewhere, and this is also the case with cyber-crime security.

Security professionals need to adopt a layered approach to their organisations' security, while endeavouring to understand where they fit into the bigger picture. This is exactly what criminals and cyber-criminals do when they are planning to commit an offence – you have to know your enemy.

Many investigators suggest that there are limitations to the information and intelligence that can be gathered in relation to cyber-crime, but there is not; there is only a need to balance, risk assess and evaluate one's ability to gather such intelligence.

REFLECTIVE TASK

In the Home Office's Police Science & Technology Strategy 2004–2009, *which can be found online at www.homeoffice.gov.uk/documents/PoliceST_S2_part112835.pdf?view= Binary, it states:*

The Government e-crime strategy, to be published soon, aims to provide a coherent, consolidated statement of the Government position across departments in relation to e-crime. It provides a framework for Government, law enforcement and industry action in response to e-crime, seeking to resolve specific questions and to focus debate on longer-term issues.

(Home Office, 2004, p18)

The e-Crime Strategy *has now been published and can be found at www.acpo.police.uk/ asp/policies/Data/Ecrime%20Strategy%20Website%20Version.pdf.*

Now analyse both documents and decide if the e-Crime Strategy *is the deliverable that the* Police Science & Technology Strategy *promised.*

Training

To fight cyber-crime successfully we all need to be continually educated, and this includes the judiciary, IT communities and those responsible for digital security. The form of training will be dictated by the position and responsibilities an individual holds within an organisation. Does training end? No; because of the ever changing pace of technological development, regular and refresher training is essential during a practitioner's career. Despite the fact that the primary basics of technology remain unchanged, the hardware and software change day by day. Potentially, fresh training will be required in all new software, to facilitate the efficient examination and gathering of electronic evidence. In reality, most of this updating is done 'on the job', but significant changes often do necessitate more dedicated training.

C H A P T E R S U M M A R Y

First, we can conclude from this chapter that, if we increase the reporting and analysis of cyber-crime, the subsequent intelligence will lead to the growth of a more secure digital environment, in which law enforcement, businesses and their stakeholders will be able to interact in the pursuit of common objectives. We have to acknowledge that there is under-reporting of cyber-crime, and this also harms our ability to gather intelligence, and to investigate and scope the problem. More importantly, we need to remember that not every computer-associated investigation is a cyber-crime.

Second, for us to successfully combat cyber-crime, we will need to see a tightening of international digital legislation and of cross-border law enforcement coordination. But as can be deduced from the content of this chapter, there also needs to be a more creative and innovative answer from the organisations under threat. Bit by bit, knee-jerk security solutions should give way to strategically deployed security systems and layered security. These collective measures and better user education are the primary safeguards against the guile and cunning of cyber-criminal activities.

Lastly, cyber-crime investigations require support and, given the jurisdictional issues, resource implications and possible scale of enquiries, it is important to have early intervention by management. This will ensure that the most appropriate lines of enquiry are taken and that parameters are clearly set, which in turn will save time and expense, and make any cyber-crime investigation effective and efficient.

REFERENCES

Chisum, Jerry and Turvey, Brent (2000) Evidence dynamics: Locard's Exchange Principle and crime reconstruction. *Journal of Behavioural Profiling*, 1(1).

Council of Europe (CoE) (2001) *Convention on Cybercrime*. Available online at http://conventions. coe.int/Treaty/en/Treaties/html/185.htm (accessed 21 January 2010).

Dodd, Vikram (2001) Mass killers. *The Guardian*, 6 January. Available online at www.guardian.co.uk/uk/ 2001/jan/06/shipman.health3 (accessed 21 January 2010).

European Information Society Group/Institute for Public Policy Research (EURIM/IPPR) (2005) *Partnership Policing for the Information Society* (press release). Available online at www.eurim.org.uk/ activities/ecrime/ecrime_cybercommunities_pr.doc (accessed 21 January 2010). The full text of the discussion paper is available online at www.eurim.org.uk/activities/ecrime/cybercommunities.doc (accessed 21 January 2010).

Home Office (2004) *Police Science & Technology Strategy 2004–2009*. London: Science Policy Unit. Available online at www.homeoffice.gov.uk/documents/PoliceST_S2_part112835.pdf?view=Binary (accessed 21 January 2010).

Mills, Elinor (2009) Study: cyber-crime cost firms $1 trillion globally. *Cnet News*, 28 January. Available online at http://news.cnet.com/8301-1009_3-10152246-83.html (accessed 21 January 2010).

National Statistics (2009) *Society: Internet access*. Available online at www.statistics.gov.uk/CCI/ nugget.asp?ID=8 (accessed 21 January 2010).

Verizon Business (2009) *Data Breach Investigations Report*. Available online at www.verzonbusiness. com/resources/security/reports/2009_databreach_rp.pdf (accessed 21 January 2010).

Young, Tom (2009) Foiling a thoroughly modern bank heist. *Computing.co.uk*, 19 March. Available online at www.computing.co.uk/computing/analysis/2238637/foiling-thoroughly-modern-bank-4523310 (accessed 21 January 2010).

· USEFUL WEBSITES

www.acpo.police.uk (Association of Chief Police Officers)

www.computing.co.uk (Computing.co.uk is an online journal)

www.homeoffice.gov.uk (Home Office, with links to crime information, the police and statistics)

www.interpol.int (Interpol)

www.justice.gov/criminal/cybercrime (Computer Crime & Intellectual Property Section, US Department of Justice)

www.statistics.gov.uk (government statistic on all aspects of society, including computer usage)

www.verizonbusiness.com (the Verizon Business website carries information on networks and IP innovation)

Computer Misuse Act 1990 (as amended by the Police and Justice Act 2006)

Criminal Justice Act 1988

Criminal Justice and Public Order Act 1994

Criminal Procedure and Investigations Act 1996

Forgery and Counterfeiting Act 1981

Fraud Act 2006

Protection of Children Act 1978

Public Order Act 1986

Sexual Offences Act 2003

4 The Internet: preventative and investigative measures

CHAPTER OBJECTIVES

By the end of this chapter you should be able to:

- understand some of the impacts that the growth of the Internet has had on law enforcement;
- describe how law enforcement has grasped online opportunities to respond to the demands of cyber-crime investigations;
- appreciate how both government and the police service have developed e-crime strategies to tackle the problem of cyber-crime on the Internet;
- analyse a number of issues related to the impact of the Internet on policing, including legislation and associated legal difficulties.

LINKS TO STANDARDS

This chapter provides opportunities for links with the following Skills for Justice, National Occupational Standards (NOS) for Policing and Law Enforcement 2008.

AE1.1	Maintain and develop your own knowledge, skills and competence.
HA1	Manage your own resources.
CO1	Identify and secure electronic evidence sources.
CO3	Capture and preserve electronic evidence.
CO4	Investigate electronic evidence.
CO5	Evaluate and report electronic evidence.
CO6	Conduct Internet investigations.
CO7	Conduct network investigations.

Introduction

This chapter explores the legislation required to carry out covert and surveillance actions on the Internet, and will expand your knowledge of cyber-crime preventative and investigative measures, especially with regard to the Internet.

This is supplemented with practical advice that highlights the growth of public surveillance on the Internet and how this has impacted on investigations. The chapter also explores some of the issues involved in the use of the Internet as an investigative tool, and includes information on how to combat cyber-crime through the use of e-crime prevention.

Despite the concerted efforts of public and private organisations, cyber-crime is growing and is highly unlikely to shrink. Those with very few principles will always find and exploit opportunities to make money and not get caught. Many forms of this criminality take place online and across the Internet.

It can be very difficult to identify the source of a message that has been sent across the Internet, and this is further complicated by the cyber-criminals who make every effort to hide their identities. Fortunately, there are techniques that have the potential to reveal details of where such messages came from and discover the identity of the cyber-criminal.

So what has caused this growth in cyber-crime through the Internet? Well, deceptions online do not cost much to establish and run; the potential audience is global; the chance of getting caught is low, as is the possibility of being prosecuted; and those organising and taking part in it are making money.

Types of Internet cyber-crime

As discussed earlier, there are many types of Internet cyber-crime, including:

- phishing;
- obfuscated URLs;
- spam;
- computer viruses and worms;
- spyware;
- malware;
- denial of service;
- and more . . ..

In particular, there are the extremists and vigilantes. The Internet provides a means for people around the world to voice their opinions and ideas. The majority of us use this freedom of expression appropriately; however, there is a minority that abuses it.

Investigation of phishing and obfuscated URLs

There is an essential need for law enforcement to provide an effective capability that can meet the demands of a rapidly changing cyber-crime arena. There is a need constantly to evaluate current and future threats and train investigators accordingly. By initially looking at these threats and applying traditional policing methodology we can establish a best working practice for investigating cyber-crime offences such as phishing and obfuscated URLs.

ISPs dealing with malicious and nuisance communications have divided email into two categories:

- unsolicited commercial email (UCE);

- email that forms part of more worrying events, for example where there is evidence of human malice specifically targeted at the victim, such as stalking, intimidation and threats.

UCE is akin to 'junk mail' and will not be a law enforcement matter. Although some UCE spam is sent unlawfully, the source of much of it is not traceable and, if it comes from abroad, there can be problems prosecuting due to the restrictions on the jurisdiction of UK courts.

What would be unlawful is where a person is in receipt of spam via the Internet, which on the face of it is attempting to elicit money from the recipient illegally. This is known as an advance fee '419' fraud (the name 419 comes from the section of the Nigerian penal code that addresses fraudulent schemes).

The victim is enticed into believing they have been singled out from the rest of society to share in a million-pound handout for doing almost next to nothing. The intended victim receives a letter, fax or email from a supposedly legitimate individual representing a foreign financial or government institution. Within the communication is an offer to transfer millions of pounds into the victim's personal bank account. If the victim wants to proceed, they have to provide personal and banking information, which has to be provided up front with a fee that will facilitate the main transfer of the monies – hence it is an advance fee fraud.

The victim should hand a copy of the full email, including header and complete sender details, to their local police. The victim should also contact their service provider to establish options open to them to prevent the receipt of further spam.

Where UCE spam received via the Internet contains the following, it should initially be reported to the Internet Watch Foundation (IWF), rather than to the police or ISP:

- images of child abuse anywhere in the world;

- adult material, received in or sent from the UK, that potentially breaches the Obscene Publications Act 1959;

- criminally racist material sent from or received in the UK.

In these cases, the IWF conducts the initial investigation into the matter to establish if and where the crime has been committed and then passes it to the relevant law enforcement agency for full investigation.

Therefore, using the above guidelines as a benchmark to avoid giving investigators unnecessary work, best practices can be established for the investigation of cyber-crime offences such as phishing and obfuscated URLs.

Whether or not the reported incident appears to be classed as a crime in England and Wales, the fact that a person has reported it will be recorded and a reference number will be given. This will reassure the person and will provide a point of contact for the exchange of information.

At this point it should be noted that, where an allegation of an offence committed on and/or facilitated by the Internet is reported to the police, they would retain ownership of the investigation until it can be correctly and properly placed.

Typically, the fraudsters behind phishing scams are located outside England and Wales, and, as they are unable to transfer money directly out of their victim's online account overseas, they need a UK intermediary.

In addition, organised crime is targeting Internet users specifically to launder money stolen from online bank accounts, where people have been duped into handing over their account details.

The loss to the victim may be relatively small, but it is believed that hundreds of thousands of pounds have been sent abroad as a result of a large number of these crimes being successfully carried out.

As with '419' frauds, the laws and legal systems in place in other jurisdictions in relation to these offences do not act as a deterrent for the criminals, who make substantial gains. However, an effective cyber-crime strategy can ensure:

- that a victim sees positive action in relation to their funds;

- that there is criminal identification and prosecution within the UK;

- that international intelligence dissemination assists in the worldwide fight against cyber-crime.

PRACTICAL TASK

- *As a result of the latest data breaches in Liechtenstein in 2008, and in Switzerland in 2010, should we not consider making a concerted effort to protect global financial markets, in particular those that are considered as 'tax havens', such as the Cayman Islands, the Channel Islands, the Isle of Man and Monaco?*

- *Are these breaches going to legitimise the theft of data from financial institutions and make such activities more profitable than offences such as phishing?*

- *The person holding the stolen data from the Swiss incident is purported to be asking £2.5 million for it, so does this mean that financial institutions will become a very popular 'target of choice'?*

Use the Internet and online search engines to research and answer the questions posed above.

- *In addition, how do you think such actions will affect law enforcement's ability to investigate and prosecute such offences?*

To get you started go online and access the following articles.

- *www.reuters.com/article/idUSLDE6191UI20100210*

- *http://news.bbc.co.uk/1/hi/business/7267111.stm*

You may have concluded from your work on the above task that the actions of the German government changed the focus of the criminal fraternity so that they can make more money and avoid prosecution, and as a consequence this may increase the difficulties that law enforcement agencies face in being able to prosecute, disrupt and dismantle organised crime.

What is Internet and network forensics?

Internet forensics involves not only a single computer and computer system, but a network that goes around the world and, as a consequence, this creates a greater challenge to the identification and prosecution of offenders. A criminal resident in Australia can use a server in the United States to steal credit card numbers from hotel point of sale management systems in Canada and Sweden.

Computer forensics has by tradition been concerned with the gathering of evidence from a host, such as a workstation or laptop computer, so there has been some disquiet in dealing with the network aspect of investigations. What the majority used to believe was that very little information was kept on a network, so an investigation of it did not merit the effort or time involved.

From a historical point of view, networks were intended to be very capable at delivering data. They were never intended to actually store data, because storage was very limited in the early days of networking. The theory was that the workstation or personal computer would always store the relevant data.

The extent of the problem

There are many causes of security breaches, such as a computer user having his or her password on a sticky note under the keyboard, a smoker picking up malicious software, known as 'malware', outside the office and then plugging it into their computer, or the default password not being changed once a new system is installed.

Passwords

What most computer users need to realise is that cyber-criminals, and in particular hackers, know the most common passwords used by the general public, and can automatically shower an online account with hundreds of predictable choices to see if any of them work.

In a recent survey, Imperva found that nearly 50 per cent of passwords were made up of exceptionally easy combinations, such as '123456', 'abc123', 'iloveyou' and 'password'.

REFLECTIVE TASK

Go to the *Imperva* report, Consumer Password Worst Practices, *which can be found at* www.imperva.com/docs/WP_Consumer_Password_Worst_Practices.pdf, *and read the article. Do any of your passwords appear there? If they do, it is strongly recommended that you change them.*

Poor passwords run the risk of being hacked by 'brute force' or 'dictionary' attacks, the latter being where a program is set up to input every word in the dictionary into the password box.

Loss of personal data

A classic example of a loss of personal data was when the confidential records of millions of British gamblers, who bet with top bookmaker Ladbrokes, were offered for sale to *The Mail on Sunday*:

> The huge data theft is now at the centre of a criminal investigation after the newspaper was given the personal information of 10,000 Ladbrokes customers and offered access to its database of 4.5 million people in the UK and abroad.
>
> (MailOnline, 2010)

Social engineering

Social engineering is the art of manipulating others into revealing sensitive information or performing actions, instead of breaking in or using hacking techniques. While similar to a confidence trick, deception or basic fraud, the term typically applies to trickery for the purpose of information gathering or computer system access. Phishing is a technique for fraudulently obtaining private information.

REFLECTIVE TASK

Go to the online article at www.dailymail.co.uk/news/article-1245622/For-sale-Personal-details-millions-Ladbrokes-gamblers.html and learn more about how the personal data in the Ladbrokes incident was put up for sale. Consider whether the public are sufficiently aware of the dangers when providing personal data to others.

E-crime prevention strategy for businesses

Small and medium enterprises

The risks to small and medium enterprises (SMEs) from, for example, 'cardholder not present' frauds are immense, as the banks charge such losses to the businesses involved.

In a ZDNet article, Jeremy Beale, head of e-business at the Confederation of British Industry (CBI), was quoted as saying:

> *As regards funding, e-crime is a problem for everyone and often impacts more than one party. Businesses would probably be prepared to pay for services of particular sectoral interest to them. But in general it should be funded out of general taxation.*
>
> (Neath, 2008)

In the same article, Catherine Bowen, head of crime policy at the British Retail Consortium (BRC), was reported as saying that businesses would expect to have input on the running of the unit if they were supporting its costs. She stated:

> *We would expect there to be consultation with our members to ensure their concerns were being properly addressed by the unit . . . We need to get away from seeing cybercrime as being synonymous with big business; it affects small businesses just as much. Small and Medium Enterprises' (SME) funding an e-crime unit is not feasible. In short, normal policing is paid for out of the public purse, therefore e-crime too.*
>
> (Neath, 2008)

There is an immense and growing influence of the Internet over everyday business activity. It has been recognised that an electronically mediated attack upon an SME may lead to significant costs or even business closure, for example 'ransomware' being maliciously installed so that it encrypts a company's data and can only be removed after payment of a ransom. This must be balanced against other considerations; for example, smaller City companies, in order to remain competitive or expand, will need to become more extensive users or adopters of electronic commercial opportunities – in other words, electronic commerce (e-commerce).

It is not unusual in small enterprises for all staff to have access to the Internet and all of the enterprise's data, and there are vast numbers of SMEs that are inadequate users of information and communication technology (ICT). Could they do more? Are they very vulnerable to cyber-crime? Should they be the subjects of e-crime prevention? One very good example of this is the National e-Crime Prevention Centre (NeCPC).

> *The National e-Crime Prevention Centre (NeCPC) is a multidisciplinary and multi-agency network and currently a virtual centre of excellence in e-Crime prevention and enterprise security. Membership from international agencies, universities, industry and crime prevention units provides a critical mass of expertise.*
>
> *Regional, national and international links are being established with agencies and leading businesses through the centre, including links with professional bodies, industry, public authorities, and academic institutions worldwide.*
>
> (NeCPC, 2010)

A large number of organisations are failing to recognise all aspects of the security risks that they are exposed to. Some do not realise the magnitude of the risk, some do not have the know-how to mitigate their vulnerability, and countless others fail to provide sufficient resources to lessen the risk.

It is therefore acceptable to conclude that, on the whole, information and data security in this level of enterprise needs to be enhanced. Numerous enterprises, particularly small firms, still need to make sizeable progress towards protecting their clients and customers from the risk of hi-tech and e-crime.

The Financial Services Agency (FSA) has stated: 'If firms fail to take account of this report and continue to demonstrate poor data security practice, we may refer them to Enforcement' (FSA, 2008).

The focus of any new strategy for the private and public sectors needs to be on e-crime prevention, and this needs to be supported by proactive and cyber-crime hi-tech investigations.

Large enterprises

The upper level of enterprises generally allocates ample resources for security risk management, but there is a need for coordination between departments, such as IT, information security, human resources, general security and fraud. Many organisations have experienced this first hand during a significant number of cyber-crime investigations.

The centre of attention for this level of organisation is on control rather than procedures, accountability, policy and due diligence. A lot of them have single points of failure when it comes to information and data security. For example, in August 2006, the BBC reported that fraudsters in West Africa were able to find Internet banking data stored on recycled personal computers sent from the UK to Africa (*BBC News*, 2006).

The FSA, in their recent report, *Data Security in Financial Services* (FSA, 2008, p74), has consolidated examples of poor practice in data security, for example:

- no training to communicate policies and procedures;

- temporary staff receiving less rigorous vetting than permanently employed colleagues carrying out similar roles;

- failing to consider continually whether employees in higher-risk positions are becoming vulnerable to committing fraud or being coerced by criminals;

- failing to monitor super-users or other employees with access to large amounts of customer data;

- allowing access to web-based communication Internet sites; this content includes web-based email, messaging facilities on social networking sites, external instant messaging and 'peer-to-peer' file-sharing software;

- slack procedures that present opportunities for fraudsters, for instance when confidential waste is left unguarded on the premises before it is destroyed;

- firms stockpiling obsolete computers and other portable media for too long and in insecure environments;

- firms relying on others to erase or destroy their hard drives and other portable media securely without evidence that this has been done competently. These areas and more could be targeted by a robust e-crime prevention approach.

REFLECTIVE TASK

Law enforcement agencies employ crime prevention officers who provide advice to the private sector, but how many e-crime prevention officers are there? Very few, so should this be changed?

Make a list of the advantages that additional e-crime prevention officers would bring. Would this be a cost-effective exercise and what knowledge base should such officers have?

Covert surveillance on the Internet

The Human Rights Act (HRA) 1998 incorporates the European Convention on Human Rights (ECHR) into domestic law and places considerations of an individual's rights to privacy at the centre of law enforcement investigations.

Impact of human rights

In all investigations the principles of legality, necessity and proportionality need to be applied to the investigative technique being adopted, as failure to do so may result in the inadmissibility of any evidence obtained.

Article 8 of the HRA guarantees rights to privacy. The intrusion into someone's right to privacy should be justifiable on the grounds of proportionality and necessity. Part 2 of the Regulation of Investigatory Powers Act (RIPA) 2000 also requires investigators to think about the degree of intrusion planned, and it should be proportionate to the seriousness of the crime under investigation. The technique adopted should also be a necessary means of achieving the desired result, and this applies to the use of surveillance to seek out private information.

Part 2 of RIPA deals with two types of covert surveillance: directed and intrusive (s26(1)). Activity is covert if it is carried out in a way that is intended to make certain that the persons who are subject to surveillance are ignorant of the fact that it is or may be taking place (s26(9)(a)).

Surveillance is intrusive if it is covert, and is carried out in relation to anything taking place on any residential premises or in any private motor vehicle, and involves the presence of an individual on that premises or in the vehicle, or is carried out by means of a surveillance device (s26(3)(a) and (b)). These are hidden electronic devices that are used to capture, record and/or transmit data to a receiving party, such as a law enforcement agency.

Surveillance is directed if it is covert, is undertaken for the purpose of a specific investigation, and is likely to result in the obtaining of private information (s26(2)(a) and (b)).

Private information in relation to a person includes any information relating to their private or family life (s26(10)). It includes an individual's relationships with others, their associates, lifestyle and finances. It is immaterial whether the person about whom the information is gathered is the subject of the investigation.

Just because the information is publicly available on the Internet, it can still be considered to be private. If it is considered likely that private information may be obtained through covert surveillance, a directed surveillance authority, which is permission to carry out such surveillance, must be obtained.

Therefore, serious consideration should be given before using an innovative or online investigative technique. Such measures need to be considered against the surveillance definitions highlighted above. This extends from the 'harvesting' of the Internet for intelligence through to covert presence within an online social networking group.

Interception of communications

Advances in technology, in particular the growth in the use of the Internet as a communication tool, have resulted in the need for legislation to allow for the interception of communications. Such an interception is a breach of article 8; however, a legal basis for breaching the article was introduced by Part 1 of RIPA.

Generally, to obtain the content of any message in the 'course of transmission' requires an interception warrant, but if the message has been sent and received, and is stored data, it can be obtained through a production order or search warrant.

Being in the course of transmission is when a communication is stored on a system for the intended recipient to access. An interception of that communication takes place where, for example, an email message stored on a web-based service provider is accessed so that its contents are made available to someone other than the sender or the intended recipient.

Property interference

We have highlighted how legislation governs the way law enforcement agencies conduct intrusive surveillance, and the same applies to entering on to, or interfering with, property, premises and vehicles. An example of such interference would be entry on to residential premises to install a 'key logger' (see below) on a suspect's computer. Not only would authority be required under Part 3 of the Police Act 1997 for the property interference, an authority for intrusive surveillance within the residential premises would also be required.

Key logging

Key logging is a means of capturing and recording keystrokes and is legitimately used by organisations to troubleshoot problems with computer and network systems. Hardware and software key loggers that are used to carry out this function are commercially available and easy to obtain on the Internet.

PRACTICAL TASK

Find out how easy it is to purchase a key logger. Go online and use a search engine such as Google, enter the words 'key logger' and others such as 'buy', and see what the

---

Policy keeping

The precise recording of decisions taken throughout the course of an investigation is vital. This is particularly the case in respect of covert investigative techniques that may breach an individual's rights under the ECHR.

The record needs to be a true, accurate and timed record of the policy decisions made, and the basis supporting those decisions will reflect the proportionality and the accountability of the investigative strategy employed. Examples of technical policy decisions include the RIPA and Police Act applications, details of analysts, key forensic personnel or specialists, principal lines of technical enquiry, investigative priorities and a forensics policy.

The existence of a policy book will be disclosed to the Crown Prosecution Service (CPS) in any legal proceedings. The contents will not automatically be disclosed to the defence, as Public Interest Immunity (PII) may be sought through the courts in respect of the contents.

At a PII application, a judge can grant a court order that allows a party involved in a case to refrain from disclosing evidence to the other or others, whereby such disclosure would be damaging to the public interest. In making such an order, the judge has to balance public interest against the administration of justice.

The majority of covert investigations will involve interference with an individual's right under article 8, and any interference with these rights will give rise to a violation of the article unless the interference was in accordance with the law and in pursuit of one or more of the legitimate aims referred to in the article, such as national security or the prevention of crime.

The application of the requirements of legality, necessity and proportionality extends across all aspects of investigative techniques. This is the test that must be applied to activities such as the insertion of a physical key logger on to a keyboard located within private premises. Failure to comply with this test will result in the possibility of a range of outcomes, from failed prosecutions to civil litigation.

Covert Internet investigators

A highly specialist role within this area of cyber-crime investigation is that of the covert Internet investigator or CII. This can be a designated role or a part-time role; the latter is usually combined with another cyber-crime duty, such as that of digital forensic investigator, and there needs to be a clear separation of duties when this occurs. In addition, clear physical and procedural segregation should be in place to separate any intelligence-related work from evidential material, in order to prevent any contamination with procedures in this area.

As stated in the ACPO *Good Practice Guide for Computer-Based Electronic Evidence* (7safe, undated), *The deployment of CIIs is governed by the National Standards in Covert Investigations*, which are detailed in the *Manual of Standards for the Deployment of Covert Internet Investigators*. However, operationally the following are some of the points that need to be considered and/or addressed in order to achieve the efficient and effective use of a CII.

- Ensure that the environment that the CII is to work in is specifically created and not allowed simply to evolve.

- Any CII should liaise with other experienced CIIs if he or she wishes to conduct unfamiliar activities on the Internet. This is to ensure that CIIs who are unfamiliar with a given area of work are provided with suitable advice in relation to best practice and terminology.

- A 'subject' may be defined as an online user who is suspected of online criminal activity and is a potential suspect in an investigation, and who is known or is not yet identified by their real name.

- CII and support personnel assigned to CII work should be given confidential access to counselling if the investigation or work and/or external conditions require them to seek support.

- Undercover activities should be limited to those areas of an online service, or the Internet, which have been previously established as a suitable environment for that area of work.

- Undercover activities conducted online should focus solely on the activities previously approved by the lead investigator and/or senior management.

- Undercover CIIs should obtain prior approval for monitoring online activities and participation.

- All undercover activities should be fully documented in their entirety and archived in an electronic format. Undercover CIIs should initiate logging procedures upon signing on to the online service or Internet. Additionally, undercover CIIs will ensure that an investigation report is prepared, documenting all undercover activity.

- It is recommended that the CIIs ensure that case law and legislation can be adhered to electronically; that is, carrying out periodic forensic imaging of the computer media in use and the methodology used to store digital records of the online sessions.

- Undercover CIIs should prepare a log containing a unique identifying reference for each session conducted. This log should contain the source of the activity, the name of the individual CII and the session number of the activity being conducted by that individual. This system will ensure that management is able to maintain an overview of activities and is able to disseminate information and intelligence where appropriate.

- No undercover CII will utilise software that is not properly registered and purchased or obtained correctly.

- The following forensic principle should be applied to all procedures employed and accountability should always be at the forefront of operational decisions.

- Principle – An audit trail or other record of all processes applied to computer-based electronic evidence should be created and preserved. An independent third party should be able to examine those processes and achieve the same result.

This list is not exhaustive, but is a fair representation of points to consider when entering into this arena of covert work. Any requests relating to online activity should be directed to an identified manager to determine if the request is justified and proportionate.

Legal considerations

Protection of information and compliance with legislation must be seen as of primary importance to all; however, as with security controls, the adoption of legislation is not keeping pace with the growing use of emerging technologies.

Legislation

The number of stated cases and new legislation go to show how Internet and computer forensics has affected numerous investigations and has provided forceful evidence for civil and criminal proceedings.

- *R v. M & Others* **[2007]**: Compact discs or other computer storage media that are capable of holding electronic data were also capable of being articles within the meaning of the Terrorism Act 2000 (s57).

- *Perry* v. *The UK* **[2003]**: This case related to human rights and involved covert video evidence that had been obtained without any appropriate authority. This concerns the issue of interference with private life in a public place. As such, it is one to be considered when dealing with investigations involving the Internet as, at present, there is no clear direction as to which areas of the Internet are public and which are to be considered private.

However, to continue to be effective, cyber-crime detection and prosecution have to be driven by information uncovered during a cyber-crime investigation, and this intelligence and evidence needs to have been acquired in line with legislation, so that it can be put before a court. There must also be nothing about how the evidence was collected and subsequently handled that casts doubt on its authenticity and veracity; in other words, it must be reliable.

Legality

There are more and more instances of electronic media of a company or an individual being networked to a server or servers. In order to be cost-effective, the server is then partitioned and used by more than one organisation. This then raises massive problems in relation to collateral intrusion and the possibility of huge legal claims against those involved in an investigation.

Because computers have such wide and varied uses within an organisation or home, there may be legal prohibitions against searching every file. A computer belonging to a solicitor, doctor or a financial adviser may contain not only evidence of a wrongdoing, but probably also information that is privileged. The same applies to data centrally stored on a server that contains incriminating evidence.

Jurisdictional differences

Different jurisdictions, and different regulatory regimes within the same jurisdiction, may deal with judicial procedures in dissimilar ways. Currently, there is no common or multi-jurisdictional standard for addressing and resolving such issues. This inconsistency presents immense challenges to those in the international business field, and a business operating in multiple countries will have to comply with a number of different, and sometimes contradictory, legal constraints. This in itself can amount to a considerable burden on an organisation, and the answer to this type of problem will largely be delivered through the actions of those involved and the decisions made by the courts and by the regulators.

Electronic discovery (e-discovery – see next paragraph) is a part of the business environ-ment that is here to stay, and will present ever greater challenges in the future as the globalisation of businesses continues to grow at a significant rate. To meet these changes and obligations, practical electronic document storage and retention policies will have to be formulated. Such a policy will need to meet the needs of an organisation in each and every jurisdiction in which it operates. Plotting a way through the various rules and how they impact on an organisation in each country can be difficult.

While not mutually exclusive, there are key differences between e-discovery, computer forensics and cyber-crime. E-discovery is a process undertaken in connection with litigation or a regulatory investigation, and seeks to identify information that is specifically responsive to a defined issue, producing electronically stored information.

In Australia, England and Wales, the litigant is required to disclose all documents upon which they rely and all documents that undermine their case. Alternatively, in the USA, adverse documents are in general not wholly produced unless they are at the centre of an official document request. The US approach at a national level is based on common law jurisdiction with lenient pre-trial discovery and is governed by the Federal Rules of Civil Procedure.

The Sarbanes–Oxley Act 2002 had a considerable impact on the data management policies of US organisations. The US position, as the paramount economic country, has meant that many organisations based outside the USA must not only abide by their own country's rules, but also the rules of the USA. The Australians certainly acknowledge the interdependence between their own jurisdiction and that of the USA by including advice for organisations on Sarbanes–Oxley in the *Australian Record Retention Manual* (IEA, 2009).

Analysis of the practical problems arising in relation to e-discovery and other related subjects can be found at the Sedona Conference website. A lot of this material is intended to complement the US Federal Rules of Civil Procedure in an attempt to establish guidelines that will address the challenges posed by electronic document production. The principles put forward within the various reports are geared towards the US legal system, and are not fully suitable for adoption in the UK. Likewise, rule making in Canada is profoundly influenced by the requirements of its neighbour and principal trading partner.

In England and Wales, certain regulators are increasingly requiring retention of specific categories of documents. The rules governing e-discovery in England and Wales are known as the Civil Procedure Rules (CPR).

REFLECTIVE TASK

Go to www.thesedonaconference.org/publications_html, and explore the available links to find out more about e-discovery. Find out how this civil process is likely to impact on a criminal investigation, identify the approaches being adopted in e-discovery, and discover how effective they are likely to be in a criminal investigation.

Forms of regulation

There are no all-encompassing Sarbanes–Oxley type rules, but if the developments in e-discovery in the USA are a sign as to what may be in store for other countries, then changes have to occur, and other countries will need to continue to develop e-discovery best practices, particularly with regard to proportionality and costs. It is now for the different legal communities to decide how to keep up with these growing changes.

The need for organisations to change rapidly, without major disruption, has led governments to seek forms of regulation that will supplement self-regulation. At this time, countries tend to fall into one of the following categories:

- low levels of regulation, reliant on self-regulation, with high levels of compliance;

- high levels of regulation, with low levels of compliance and, as a consequence, no real means of enforcement.

What they do all agree on is that regulation is ineffective in the absence of compliance or certification. An organisation that fails to take on a recognised regulation that includes incident response, or adopts just a 'patch and go' approach, is going to fall short of business best practices in relation to information security management.

This chapter will have provided you with information and resources to assist with your studies and will have opened up some areas for debate, especially around e-crime prevention and the covert policing of the Internet.

Knowledge and understanding of e-discovery and Internet abuse continue to grow. Some cases develop into major civil and criminal prosecutions, causing considerable difficulties if the legislation and principles for seizing and producing evidence have not been applied. Thorough and accurate implementation of these principles from the outset will provide the best opportunity for a successful investigation.

Unfortunately, for many the investigative processes are either non-existent or merely consist of attempting to work with a substandard set of policies and procedures. However, changes are taking place and fast. The NPIA is developing high-quality training solutions for such operatives as CIIs, and a modular training programme has been developed to meet the needs of law enforcement and to support the *ACPO e-Crime Strategy*. All of which goes towards giving increased ability to law enforcement agencies to combat cyber-crime and the criminal use of technology.

This chapter has provided you with an overview of Internet policing, in particular the online investigation aspect of cyber-crime, online surveillance, e-crime prevention and the influence of legislation on them. Opportunities have been provided for further research and a number of controversial subjects have been considered, such as how law enforcement agencies need to justify breaching a person's privacy and human rights. Further reading and research will help to develop some of the information presented.

REFERENCES

BBC News (2006) UK Bank details sold in Nigeria. *BBC News*, 14 August. Available online at http://news.bbc.co.uk/1/hi/business/4790293.stm (accessed 7 February 2010).

Financial Services Authority (FSA) (2008) *Data Security in Financial Services*. London: FSA. Available online at www.fsa.gov.uk/pubs/other/data_security.pdf (accessed 7 February 2010).

Information Enterprises Australia (IEA) (2009) *Australian Record Retention Manual.* Fremantle, WA: IEA.

MailOnline (2010) For sale: personal details of millions of Ladbrokes gamblers offered to the MoS by a mysterious Australian. *MailOnline*, 24 January. Available online at www.dailymail.co.uk/news/article-1245622/For-sale-Personal-details-millions-Ladbrokes-gamblers.html (accessed 31 March 2010).

National e-Crime Prevention Centre (NeCPC) (2010) *Welcome to the NeCPC*. Available online at http://necpc.org.uk (accessed 7 February 2010).

Neath, Nick (2008) Businesses may be forced to fund e-crime unit. ZDNet UK, 18 March. Available online at http://news.zdnet.co.uk/security/0,1000000189,39369101,00.htm (accessed 7 February 2010).

7safe (undated) ACPO *Good Practice Guide for Computer-Based Electronic Evidence:* Official release version. Available online at www.7safe.com/electronic_evidence/ACPO_guidelines_computer_evidence.pdf (accessed 10 May 2010).

www.fsa.gov.uk (Financial Services Authority)

www.iwf.org.uk/ (Internet Watch Foundation)

www.necpc.org.uk (National e-Crime Prevention Centre)

www.npia.police.uk/ (National Policing Improvement Agency)

Perry v. The UK – 63737/00 [2003] ECHR 375 (17 July 2003)

R v. M and Others (No. 1) [2007] EWCA Crim 218

R v. M and Others (No. 2) [2007] EWCA Crim 970; [2007] 3 All ER 53

Human Rights Act 1998

Obscene Publications Act 1959

Police Act 1997

Privacy and Electronic Communications Regulations 2003

Regulation of Investigatory Powers Act 2000

Sarbanes–Oxley Act 2002

Terrorism Act 2000 (s57)

UK Civil Procedure Rules

US Federal Rules of Civil Procedure

5 The use of forensics in combating crime

CHAPTER OBJECTIVES

By the end of this chapter you should be able to:

- understand computer forensics and digital evidence;
- describe the roles of computer specialists and experts;
- outline how to collect evidential data;
- describe the forensic examination of computer media;
- understand the cyber-crime policing strategy and the associated legislation;
- analyse a number of key issues relating to the use of computer forensics and its contribution to crime investigations.

LINKS TO STANDARDS

This chapter provides opportunities for links with the following Skills for Justice, National Occupational Standards (NOS) for Policing and Law Enforcement 2008.

CO1   Identify and secure electronic evidence sources.
CO2   Seize and record electronic evidence sources.
CO3   Capture and preserve electronic evidence.
CO4   Investigate electronic evidence.
CO5   Evaluate and report electronic evidence.

Computer forensics is a relatively new discipline and, in this chapter, we will address the ever increasing use of computer technology to combat crime. It will provide an understanding of the digital evidence that can be abstracted from a computer and used in an investigative role. The chapter will assist students in how to face the challenge of understanding both computer forensic technologies and the principles and practices of cyber-crime investigation. Global case studies will be introduced to show how this type of investigation has already produced some interesting situations.

Introduction

The expression 'computer forensics' was first used back in 1991 in a training session held by the International Association of Computer Investigation Specialists (IACIS) in Portland, Oregon (New Technologies, undated), and is generally accepted as being a captivating subject. It has been used comprehensively for technology-related investigations and intelligence gathering by law enforcement and military agencies since the 1980s. Nevertheless, this form of investigation is somewhat new within the private sector, but it has grown in use and acceptability as a result of the rising regularity of hi-tech crime and the ever rising cost of 'cyber-liability'.

Cyber-crime, hi-tech crime or e-crime, whatever words you use, has no boundaries, particularly in relation to jurisdiction. What is constant is that such crime is committed over a computer network and these networks have generated a new cyberworld, complete with its own communities, systems, languages and cultures. Of course, the biggest network of all is the Internet.

To understand computer forensics, we really first need to ask the question, 'What is hi-tech crime?' Cyber-crime has become a rapidly growing phenomenon over recent years. Computers, and in particular the Internet, provide great benefits for society. However, there is a real threat that criminals will exploit these mediums, turning a tool designed to benefit society into a tool to help them commit crime. Cyber-crime encompasses a variety of criminal activity. As explained earlier in the book, first there are 'new crimes, new tools' – new crimes committed against computers and IT networks that present new opportunities to criminals and new challenges to investigators, for example hacking and spoof websites. The second type of cyber-crime is 'new tools, old crimes' – traditional crimes supported by the use of the Internet and hi-technology, such as fraud, blackmail and identity theft.

Additionally, it has to be remembered that the area of cyber-crime is not confined to criminal investigations; there are others such as employment disputes and breaches of company policy. It can all be described as 'computer-enabled abuse', but whatever the title, if it is not investigated properly, it can and does cause significant problems.

If an incident occurs and a company is asked to bring into being dependable digital evidence of what went on within its computer system, say after a suspected crime or attack, how well could they respond? In a document entitled *Directors and Corporate Advisors Guide to Digital Investigation and Evidence*, Peter Sommer states: 'Nearly all organisations underestimate how often they may be called on to produce reliable evidence of what has happened in and around their systems' (2005, p9).

Although slightly dated, it still applies today, and means that there is a significant problem facing us all in how best to understand the complex and dynamic developments in this ever evolving world of digital information. If we do not invest in the skills necessary to investigate this environment, we will have to contend with playing 'catch-up' in understanding how new technologies are associated with a range of traditional wrongdoings.

This becomes much more significant when you consider, as described earlier in the book, that the global cost of cyber-crime is now estimated to be well over one trillion dollars a year (Mills, 2009), and this type of crime has no regional, national or international boundaries, unlike law enforcement, which has physical and remit boundaries, and limits in relation to jurisdiction. We therefore need to make sure that we not only understand computer forensics, but that we also know how to use it as a tool in our armoury to combat crime.

What is computer forensics?

Computer forensics is a science that involves the discovery, identification, preservation, recovery, documentation and analysis of computer-stored data, which are then presented as evidence. However, some say that it is more of an art than a science, and the modus operandi for this art follows well-defined and clear methodologies. Investigators need an understanding of computers and forensics, and it is recommended that they treat all investigations as if they were going to court – civil or criminal. This makes precise documentation a crucial part of any computer-related investigation.

So, computer forensics involves the analysis of data on a computer or computer system to ascertain what an individual or individuals were doing in the cyberworld. In other words, it is the logical application of methodical investigatory techniques to discover and solve acts of digital and computer-enabled abuse.

An example of such abuse can be found in a patent infringement case, *First USA Bank* v. *PayPal* [2003], in which the plaintiff subpoenaed the defendant's former Chief Executive Officer (CEO) in an effort to forensically inspect a laptop. The outcome was a ruling in favour of the plaintiff, which authorised a forensic duplication of the laptop computer system's hard drive.

The growing problem of this type of abuse and crime is that such an act can be committed *on* any computer *from* any computer in the world, and the subsequent investigations can range from fraud to intellectual property theft to denial of service attacks.

The methodology of computer forensics

Evidence must be acquired without altering or damaging the original. The recovered digital evidence is authenticated to show that it is the same as the original, and then the analysis of the data follows in order to locate and produce digital evidence. The methodology of an investigation will depend on the circumstances and the investigative objectives; however, the steps to achieve this are always consistent.

To collect the physical evidence, law enforcement agencies use powers of search and seizure, that is, a search warrant, which is a legal document allowing a specified location to be searched for evidence relating to an offence. In the corporate world, permission is sought from the owner of a system or via a civil search warrant, known as an 'Anton Piller order'.

However, individuals in the judiciary are facing extreme challenges to their technical awareness when it comes to digital evidence. Locating, reviewing and managing such data requires knowledge of technology that often goes further than that of the most skilled user and such evidence is frequently challenged in court. Some judiciary allow it because they want to have an impact on those who use the computer to facilitate or commit a crime. In the USA, some snub it because they cling to what some believe is a technophobic view of the Fourth Amendment:

> *The right of the people to be secure in their persons, houses, papers, and effects, against unreasonable searches and seizures, shall not be violated, and no warrants shall issue, but upon probable cause, supported by oath or affirmation, and particularly describing the place to be searched, and the persons or things to be seized.*

(Free Dictionary, 2010)

What is generally accepted in the standard areas of a cyber-crime investigation is to identify, secure and seize digital evidence, to document all digital evidence, and to evaluate, investigate and report findings. In summary, we can say that computer forensics deals with the application of law to a science.

The *New Shorter Oxford English Dictionary* defines 'computer forensics' as: 'The application of forensic science techniques to computer-based material' (Oxford Dictionaries, 2007). In other words, forensic computing is the method of identifying, preserving, analysing and presenting digital evidence in a way that is up to standard for legal proceedings, and the use of this science is, in the opinion of many, one of the best ways in which cyber-crime and computer-enabled abuse can be combated.

REFLECTIVE TASK

Go to www.acpo.police.uk/asp/policies/Data/Ecrime%20Strategy%20Website%20Version.pdf, to find the ACPO *e-Crime Strategy. Read through the report and consider the options suggested for the development and use of computer forensics and how this may impact on the future of both policing and the private sector.*

One of the things you will have found is the fact that it is intended to develop strategies for forensic search, retrieval, seizure and examination, and the analysis process of digital forensics, as well as a forensic triage process. These strategies will mean that more and more law enforcement and private sector investigators will need an understanding of how computer forensics works with regard to a whole array of digital storage media.

Computers and external media

There is a wide assortment of computer storage media available and the storage space on such media continues to grow. It is predicted that, in the near future, home computers will have the capacity to store more data than servers presently used by organisations, which will mean longer retrieval and analysis times for investigators.

Currently, the amount of analysis involved in each investigation is not essentially governed by the seriousness of the abuse or offence. The recovery of data in connection with a murder may be relatively straightforward compared with that of a theft. The aim of an investigation can be as simple as identifying an email that has been sent, or as difficult as recovering deleted data in a large and intricate fraud investigation, which in turn can be complicated further with encryption.

When conducting an analysis of computer media, every effort should be made to eliminate requests such as 'Can you take a quick look?' All media submitted for analysis should go through an authorising process to assist in filtering out unnecessary requests. There is concern, however, that in many cases this authorisation may develop to be little more than a nod through. Any investigation involving digital media needs to apply itself to the 'evidence-gathering doctrine':

> *The onus is on the prosecution to show to the court that the evidence produced is no more and no less now than when it was first taken into the possession of the police.*
>
> (7safe, undated, p4)

As a consequence of this, case law has emerged in relation to the gathering of computer data for intelligence and evidential purposes. In the case of *Gates Rubber Co.* v. *Bando Chemical Indus. Ltd* (1996), the court criticised the plaintiff for failing to make image copies and for failing to properly preserve undeleted files. This highlights the fact that, on occasions, there is a duty to utilise the method that would yield the most complete and accurate results.

Computer specialists or experts

All of those involved in computer forensics have to deal with an unrivalled rate of change; nevertheless, they still have to make every effort to work to the same standards of precise authentication that are accepted in other forensic disciplines. As a consequence, the judiciary has turned to computer forensic experts and specialists for help in cutting through the technical issues that often cloud evidential objectives.

What is a specialist witness?

Specialists are likely to make witness statements that are made for different reasons and for different people to read. These provide the basis for the original evidence that specialists may give to formal proceedings, civil or criminal. In certain circumstances, all or part of a statement may be read in the absence of the specialist. A non-technical person should understand such a statement, and it should provide others who are working for a third party with a synopsis of the technical findings. A specialist is not always required to draw conclusions. If any are drawn, they should always be reinforced by factual argument in the main body of any report or statement, and in certain proceedings they may give grounds for a court to attribute expert status to the specialist.

What is an expert witness?

These types of witnesses mainly carry out their role in civil litigation, where their key function is to express highly independent expert opinion based on the information that is provided, while their key duty is to assist the court, and this overrides any obligation to the parties involved. In England and Wales, they can be appointed by one party in a dispute or appointed by both parties.

Expert computer witnesses need be qualified to analyse evidence and give a skilled view on what that evidence means. They also need to be able to make clear their findings in a graspable and concise manner, as well as being able to dispute plainly, logically and credibly any incorrect information a third party may put forward. A summary of conclusions is also obligatory and should be at the end of any report or statement.

Forensic qualifications

Currently, anyone can assert that they are qualified as an independent computer forensic expert, and recently one such expert was under investigation (*Leicester Mercury*, 2009). Despite this, it is widely accepted that experts have a responsibility to apply level-headed proficiency and care to those instructing them, and to act in accordance with any applicable professional code. They do not have a duty to act as intermediaries between parties or to impinge on the role of any formal proceedings in deciding facts, and they should point out where particular questions or areas of contention fall outside their expertise.

Neglect by an expert to conform, or unwarranted delay by the expert, may result in the instructing parties being penalised in costs or being disallowed from producing experts' evidence into the proceedings. Cost orders can also be made against the expert when he or she has disregard for the duties to the court (see the case of *Phillips* v. *Symes* [2004]). To be an expert or a specialist requires an understanding of investigations, law, computers, networks and professional certification.

There are several non-proprietary computer forensics certifications available. In some countries, such as the USA, a computer forensic specialist or expert has to have a professional certification or a private investigator's licence. Also, computer forensic software companies offer product-specific certifications, such as the Encase Certified Examiner (EnCE) certification from Guidance Software and the AccessData ACE certification.

What we can say is that the roles of an expert and a specialist are different; however, what is constant to both roles is the fact that they must have the correct qualifications and training. What they produce from a forensic examination should be comprehensive and precise. The ensuing report or statement should be written for the proposed audience and the preservation of documentation should be consistent with organisational policies, procedures, guidelines and best practices.

PRACTICAL TASK

Go to the Home Office website http://police.homeoffice.gov.uk/publications/operational-policing/practitioner-reg-summary?view=Binary and view the responses in relation to experts in the forensic science regulator's consultation paper on 'A review of the options for the accreditation of forensic practitioners'. Compare and evaluate the negative and positive aspects of the responses.

Collection of evidential data

Individuals and organisations function in multiple locations and make use of diverse types of technologies, so it can be hard to establish where any digital evidence is likely to be found. It is, therefore, essential to collect detailed information concerning the configuration of an individual's or organisation's computer system(s).

Mistakes were made in the past with regard to investigations that involved computer media and, as a result, digital evidence was lost, destroyed or compromised. However, many are now starting to utilise digital evidence more widely and fully appreciate the implications that such evidence might have for the outcome of an investigation.

The seizure of relevant digital evidence involves the identification and examination of data that could be pertinent to an investigation, and the production of evidence to aid case investigators, legal teams and the judiciary. When the evidential gathering procedures have been concluded, the actual physical collection of the relevant media and data should commence.

Those investigating need to have the ability to find digital evidence from various places within a computer or a computer system. Then, in order for it to be used successfully, the evidence must have been collected, processed and preserved in the appropriate manner. Once it has been preserved and can no longer be destroyed, an assessment of the evidence can be commenced. The procedure for this should identify a number of significant areas where the potential evidence will be located.

- **Active data**: This is electronic data that is readily on hand and available to users. This type of data includes text documents, spreadsheets and emails. This data can be easily viewed by a number of methodologies.

- **Residual data**: This is electronic data that appears to have gone from the system; however, with the use of forensic tools, the entirety of a drive can be searched and any such data, if still present, can be recovered. The quantity and type of residual data that can be recovered will vary. In the case of a partially overwritten file, the file or file fragments may also be recovered. Can deleted data be recovered? Yes – in most operating systems, the term 'deleted' does not mean destroyed; instead, when a file is deleted the computer makes the disk space occupied by that file available for new data.

- **Data evaluation**: This involves the review of data in relation to other evidence in an investigation, the drawing of deductions, the consideration of alternative conclusions and the expression of opinions. Some of the most telling evidence may be found where there is an attempt to hide or destroy data.

REFLECTIVE TASK

There are best practice principles with regard to the recovery and presentation of digital-based evidence – ACPO Good Practice Guide for Computer-Based Electronic Evidence *(7safe, undated). One of the critical ingredients of a witness statement is to show that these principles have been followed. They can be found online at www.7safe.com/electronic_evidence/ACPO_guidelines_computer_evidence.pdf (7safe, undated, p4).*

Some argue that validation, consistency, reliability and acceptance are not addressed by the current ACPO principles, and have put forward an expansion of the said principles to read as follows.

- *No action taken should change original data held on a computer/other storage media (Current ACPO Principle 1).*

- *Current ACPO Principle 2.*

- *Current ACPO Principle 3.*

- *The provider will be able to demonstrate that all tools, techniques and methods are fit for purpose.*

- *Current ACPO Principle 4 (but delete '(the case officer)').*

- *An individual is responsible for all actions taken with respect to digital evidence while the digital evidence is in their possession.*

Compare and contrast both sets of principles and consider the question 'Should forensic examiners and laboratories verify and validate every tool they use?'

Evidence

As illustrated by the principles listed above, the methods used to collect evidence should be transparent, those investigating should be ready to replicate accurately the methods used, and a third party should be able to repeat the same results. This procedure represents a significant effort, especially with the increasing size of hard drives and memory capacities, and the greater use of sophisticated Internet and computer techniques by those who commit abuse and crimes using a computer or computer systems.

If you are even slightly concerned that digital evidence will end up in civil or criminal proceedings, it is essential that a true forensic acquisition is performed. This will mean that a forensic image will be unchallengeable so long as those acquiring it follow proper procedures.

Computer forensics is having a remarkable impact on all types of investigation and there is a greater than ever growth in demand for forensic computer evidence recovery; particularly since, like any other business record, electronically stored files are discoverable in litigation, or are part of the disclosure or evidential process.

Acquiring the evidence

Digital evidence, by its very character, is unstable and can be changed or destroyed easily. This can also occur as a result of improper handling or examination. For that reason, particular precautions should be taken to ensure that this does not happen. Failure to do so may cause the evidence to be inadmissible or may lead to inaccurate conclusions. You therefore need to consider all of the following and more.

- The method of collection of physical and logical digital media.

- Corroborating your actions, for example taking photographs were appropriate.

- Ensuring a suitable evidential record is made and that the continuity of any evidence is maintained.

- The safe transportation of the evidence to where the forensic examination will take place, for example a forensic laboratory.

- Ensuring that an investigative record and a case management record are established.

- Making sure that the computer forensics workstation and any other computer media are prepared in line with accepted procedures.

- Testing the write-protection equipment that is to be used to preserve and protect the original evidence.

- Ensuring that a qualified person makes the forensic copy of the original image, and verifies the same.

In relation to the last point, the ACPO guidelines and law enforcement in general advocate a policy of dual validation. This is to ensure that no data is missed during the forensic examination of electronic media, and is achieved by the use of two forensic software tools (ACPO, 2004, p98).

Forensic examinations

These are at present examinations conducted within facilities that range from poor to excellent. However, regardless of where they are conducted, a valid and steadfast forensic examination is essential. This prerequisite recognises no physical, political, financial, technological, or jurisdictional boundaries.

Extraction of digital evidence

Extraction refers to the retrieval of data from the computer media under investigation, while analysis refers to the interpretation of the recovered data. The results obtained from either of these steps may not be adequate to draw conclusions that are right and proper. However, when the results are viewed in their entirety, they may provide a more comprehensive picture. There are practical examples of this in English law; for example, a legal test has been produced in relation to the age of a child, in proceedings under any legislation relating to indecent photographs of children. An individual is to be taken as having been a child at any material time if it appears, from the evidence as a whole, that he or she was then under the age of 18 (Protection of Children Act 1978). Other legislation (Sexual Offences Act 2003) defines a child as one under the age of 18 years or where the principal impression conveyed is that the individual shown is a child, despite having some of the physical features of an adult. However, the age of a child is ultimately for the jury to agree on. It is a finding of fact for the jury, and expert evidence is inadmissible on the subject, because it is not an issue that requires the assistance of experts (*Regina* v. *Land* [1998]).

Exhibits

Exhibits are 'real' evidence, examples of which in cyber-crime are the computers themselves, printouts of files present on computer media, file names, dates and times. These should be produced and referenced in a statement or report. The main reason for producing exhibits is for legal proceedings as well as serving a functional task for third parties. In general, they are used to help us understand the evidence and to lend a hand in explaining facts to a third party.

To ensure we have the right exhibit, we have to give each one a unique reference. The purpose of this is to individually identify an item of evidence that is referred to in a statement or report. Around the UK and the world there is a variety of methods that are used for referencing exhibits. In general, simple systems should be adopted in preference to intricate ones. In this way any individual can quickly see what an exhibit is, where it came from and its history of owners.

Continuity of evidence

Continuity of evidence has to be considered when one is preparing for, or involved in, a computer investigation. Also known as the 'chain of custody' in other parts of the world, it refers to the ability to account for everything that has taken place to an evidential exhibit, from the point of seizure or creation, to when it is presented at formal pro-ceedings. The purpose of such a process is to limit the opportunities for contamination and prove its authenticity. However, as the legal community becomes more knowledgeable about the issues surrounding electronic discovery (e-discovery) and disclosure in civil and criminal investigations, it will look for such contamination and proof of authenticity.

E-discovery is the collection, research, evaluation and production of electronic documents in litigation. This includes email and other data stored on a computer, network, backup or other storage media. Therefore, given the very nature of digital evidence, a common defence is to try to convince those presiding over any proceedings that the data have been tampered with. As a result, it is essential that mistakes do not happen. For example, the continuity of evidence must be maintained at all times and all those involved must be able to demonstrate how the evidence was discovered, how it was handled and everything that happened to it. In other words, there must be accountability. For that reason, the following questions need to be asked and answered.

- Where, when, and by whom was the evidence discovered and seized?

- Where, when and by whom was the evidence handled and/or examined?

- Who had custody of the evidence, during what period and how was it stored?

- What procedures were followed in working with the evidence?

- When and where did the evidence change custody, and how did the transfer occur?

- How can it be shown that any analysis of a copy image would be identical to that of the original evidence?

The forensic integrity of digital evidence should give us concern, because it necessitates a stringent adherence to the procedures for gathering data using a forensically sound procedure. It is absolutely necessary to maintain a record in order to show that the integrity of collected data has not been compromised and that its locality and ownership can be accounted for. The ability of electronic data to disclose powerful evidence is clear; however, the gathering of it needs to be carried out in a progressive and disciplined manner.

Inclusive and precisely documented procedures will guarantee that digital evidence is authenticated in any subsequent proceedings, and hard work at the start of any investigation will ensure that any subsequent process will run without any hiccups. We can see, therefore, that we need efficient and effective action plans for the collection or seizing of digital evidence, a fact that is critical if an investigation is to run smoothly.

This means that we should always look to improve and review our procedures by asking the following questions.

- How could the investigator's role in the investigation be improved?

- Were the results found expected?

- Did the investigation develop in the predicted manner?

- Was the documentation as thorough as it could have been?

- What feedback has been received from those involved?

- Were there any new problems?

- Was there any use of new techniques and/or technology?

- Is there a need for a review of any policy, procedure, guideline or best practice?

Notwithstanding the relative infancy of the law, digital evidence is frequently being produced in proceedings and is having a weighty impact in many investigations. This and all of the above clearly show that, if evidence collection is done in the approved manner, it will be much more useful in the investigation of crime.

Implementation of a general set of policies, procedures and best practices will also ensure the continuity and smooth transfer of digital evidence from the corporate environment to that of law enforcement, in the event that a civil investigation turns into a criminal one. You should always assume that an investigation is going to be a criminal one, otherwise such evidence might be of no value. To ensure that all parties have confidence in the results obtained, there must be a standard of acceptability that can be applied to the digital artefacts that are produced by computer forensics.

Danger areas

The answer to any hi-tech investigation is data. Without accurate reliable data there is no evidence and, without evidence, the abuser or offender cannot be brought to justice. Such data are exceptionally fragile; even switching on a computer has the potential to destroy or damage crucial data.

In digital forensics, some forms of recovery are straightforward, while others may entail high levels of expertise or new knowledge. It also has to be remembered that, when you gather digital evidence, it is recommended that you start with the volatile and work towards the less volatile. At the same time, you must ensure that digital evidence has all the attributes of other types of evidence.

Privacy-protection utilities

The hi-tech criminal fraternity is using an array of sophisticated Internet and computer techniques, as are some in the private sector. For example, in an attempt to avoid e-discovery in *iTrade Finance Inc*. v. *Webworx Inc*. in Canada in 2005, the plaintiff moved for a judgment of contempt of court based on non-disclosure of a laptop and the use of Evidence Eliminator to destroy data on the laptop when it was eventually produced. The court found for contempt. The web page for this software makes mention of forensic tools such as EnCase, and claims that their product can successfully counter these forensic software products.

Forensic crime scene contamination

A recurring theme is the number of times that victims, witnesses and some investigators have caused problems by contaminating digital evidence. Classically, an incident occurs and someone authorises the IT department to take a look. As the IT staff are actively trying to find the 'smoking gun' and save the organisation valuable down time, they are also changing the dates and times of the files that they are accessing, and are changing information that indicates who did what and when. For example, the booting up of a typical Windows operating system changes the dates and times on hundreds of files. While it may not completely put in doubt the investigation, additional hours will have to be spent on the forensic examination to explain the contamination.

Typical evidential failings

An organisation discovers potential evidence on a far-flung website and decides that it is required for evidential purposes. It could be as a result of an online transaction, or it could be a defamatory post on a social networking website. How does that organisation capture it? There are a number of ways, but many will result in post-capture modification of content.

In such a situation there are also some limitations that we need to consider. First, what can be seen on screen is not automatically what is present on the remote site, due to the Internet browser temporarily storing data, which is known as a *caching*. Second, what is being seen on screen may have been assembled from a number of sources, and in quite intricate ways. All this means that the capturing of such information, and the writing of any accompanying report or statement, needs to be done with care so that it can withstand third-party scrutiny.

REFLECTIVE TASK

Consider how to reduce contamination and improve the seizure of electronic evidence by those who are not trained in computer forensics. Make a list of points that you think should be included in an electronic crime scene procedure. Compare your answers with information provided in the ACPO Good Practice Guide for Computer-Based Electronic Evidence at www.7safe.com/electronic_evidence/ACPO_guidelines_computer_evidence.pdf.

CHAPTER SUMMARY

In this chapter you have been shown the special measures that are required when conducting an investigation that involves computer forensics, and how to use the results successfully in any formal proceedings. One of the most important measures is to make sure that the evidence has been correctly collected, and that there is clear continuity from the scene of the crime to the investigator, to the forensic examiner, and then to being presented in court as digital evidence:

> *If there is even the slightest chance that you may prosecute an individual or organisation based on evidence obtained during your forensic investigation, I highly recommend that you obtain assistance from qualified forensic analysts and/or technology minded law enforcement officers.*

(Chappell, undated)

This subject area has far-reaching implications, particularly with regard to the investigation of crime. It also emphasises the need to assume that digital evidence should be dealt with as if it were criminal: what is clear is that the procedures, techniques and guidelines examined to date are equally applicable to the collection and examination of digital evidence in internal, civil and criminal investigations.

Any digital evidence offered by any party must take full account of the implications of its integrity, validity and source. Even though computers are now an integral part of day-to-day life, we find that there is still a void between the legal and technical worlds that needs to be closed. We all need to become more aware of the implications of computer forensics and digital evidence.

Within this chapter, information has been provided with regard to a number of factors affecting computer forensics; further reading and research will give you an even more detailed understanding of how it can be used to investigate crime successfully.

REFERENCES

Association of Chief Police Officers (ACPO) (2004) *ACPO Advice and Good Practice Guide for Managers of Hi-Tech/Computer Crime Units*, ASIN: B001P9MGP2. London: Home Office Communication Directorate.

Association of Chief Police Officers (ACPO) (2009) *ACPO e-Crime Strategy*. London: ACPO.

Chappell, Laura (undated) *Introduction to Network and Local Forensics*. Available online at www.packet-level.com/pdfs/TUT186-Forensics.pdf (accessed 16 November 2009).

Forensic Science Regulator (Rennison, Andrew) (2009) Summary of the responses received for the forensic science regulator's consultation paper on 'A review of the options for the accreditation of forensic practitioners'. Available online at http://police.homeoffice.gov.uk/publications/operational-policing/practitioner-reg-summary?view=Binary (accessed 15 November 2009).

Free Dictionary (2010) *Fourth Amendment*. Available online at http://legal-dictionary.thefree dictionary.com/Fourth+Amendment (accessed 22 March 2010).

Leicester Mercury (2009) Police chief defiant over court order. *Leicester Mercury*, 28 May. Available online at www.thisisleicestershire.co.uk/news/Police-chief-defiant-court-order/article-1030724-detail/article.html (accessed 29 March 2010).

Mills, Elinor (2009) Study: cyber-crime cost firms $1 trillion globally. Cnet News, 28 January. Available online at http://news.cnet.com/8301-1009_3-10152246-83.html (accessed 21 January 2010).

New Technologies, Inc. (NTI) (undated) *Computer Forensics Defined*. Available online at www.forensics-intl.com/def4.html (accessed 14 November 2009).

Oxford Dictionaries (2007) Computer forensics, in *Shorter Oxford English Dictionary*. Oxford: Oxford University Press.

7safe (undated) *ACPO Good Practice Guide for Computer-Based Electronic Evidence: Official release version*. Available online at www.7safe.com/electronic_evidence/ACPO_guidelines_computer_evidence.pdf (accessed 15 November 2009).

Sommer, Peter (2005) *Directors and Corporate Advisors' Guide to Digital Investigations and Evidence*. Cambridge: Information Assurance Advisory Council. Available online at www.iaac.org.uk/Portals/0/Evidence%20of%20Cyber-Crime%20v08.pdf (accessed 16 November 2009).

USEFUL
WEBSITES

http://secure.evidence-eliminator.com/ (Evidence Eliminator software)

www.accessdata.com/ (AccessData, a pioneer in digital investigations)

www.acpo.police.uk/policies.asp (the 'Policies' section of the Association of Chief Police Officers' website)

www.guidancesoftware.com/ (Guidance Software, which provides computer forensics solutions for business and government)

www.iacis.org/ (International Association of Computer Investigation Specialists)

www.ojp.usdoj.gov/nij/topics/technology/electronic-crime/welcome.htm (US National Institute of Justice information on electronic crime)

www.opsi.gov.uk (Office of Public Sector Information, which has links to legislation)

CASES

First USA Bank v. PayPal, Inc. [2003] U.S. App. LEXIS 18875 (Fed. Cir. Aug. 21, 2003)

Gates Rubber Co. v. Bando Chemical Indus. Ltd, 167 F.R.D. 90, 112 (D. Colo. 1996)

iTrade Finance Inc. v. Webworx Inc. [2005]

Phillips v. Symes [2004] EWHC 2330 (Ch)

Regina v. Land [1998] 1 Cr.App.R. 301, CA

Anti-terrorism, Crime and Security Act 2001

Communications Act 2003

Computer Misuse Act 1990 (as amended by the Police and Justice Act 2006)

Criminal Justice Act 1988

Criminal Justice and Public Order Act 1988

Criminal Justice and Public Order Act 1994

Data Protection Act 1998

Forgery and Counterfeiting Act 1981

Fraud Act 2006

Proceeds of Crime Act 2002

Protection of Children Act 1978

Public Order Act 1986

Sexual Offences Act 2003

For additional information in relation to legislation not listed, you can go to the Office of Public Sector Information (OPSI), at www.opsi.gov.uk.

6 The use of CCTV in contemporary investigation

CHAPTER OBJECTIVES

By the end of this chapter you should be able to:

- describe the historical development of closed-circuit television (CCTV) within the UK;
- understand the legislation and codes of practice that relate directly to the use of CCTV systems;
- appreciate the standards required for the use of CCTV evidence within the investigative process;
- analyse a number of key issues relating to the use of CCTV within modern-day society and its implications for privacy.

LINKS TO STANDARDS

This chapter provides opportunities for links with the following Skills for Justice, National Occupational Standards (NOS) for Policing and Law Enforcement 2008.

AE1.1	Maintain and develop your own knowledge, skills and competence.
CI101.1	Conduct priority and volume investigations.
CI301	Retain, record, review and reveal material in criminal cases.
CI302	Manage property secured during operational activity.
HA1	Manage your own resources.
HA2	Manage your own resources and professional development.

Introduction

This chapter will provide you with an overview of the key legislation and codes of practice relating to the capture and use of CCTV evidence within the criminal justice system (CJS). It will also examine the growth of CCTV in our towns and cities, exploring the balance between the rights of individuals to go about their business in private and the right of the state to interfere with this in the interests of community safety and in tackling the problems of crime and disorder.

In the UK, the use of CCTV as a means of surveillance is widespread within both the public and private sectors. Citizens are now filmed and recorded on a daily basis as they go about their business and the UK has more CCTV cameras per person than anywhere else in the world (Information Commissioner, 2009).

It was during the 1960s that the video recorder and videotape started to emerge, providing a cheap and simple method of recording images without the need for a chemical process to develop images from film. This provided the user with an immediate playback facility and the potential to monitor images within centralised control rooms.

In 1960, the Metropolitan Police were the first to use CCTV in Trafalgar Square, London, to monitor crowds and, in 1961, a CCTV system was installed at a London Transport train station. The 1960s saw the emergence of other national CCTV systems, for example covert cameras in Liverpool city centre (1964), and in Dagenham, where British Railways used cameras to watch tracks that had been vandalised (1965). In 1967, Photoscan became the first company to offer a CCTV system to the retail sector as a means to deter and apprehend shoplifters.

The 1970s saw the first installation of cameras to monitor traffic in London. In 1975, video surveillance was used at a football match for the first time, and cameras were introduced in London Underground train stations. The 1980s saw further growth of the use of CCTV in cities and towns and, by 1996, all major cities in England, except Leeds, had installed CCTV systems monitoring public spaces. It was during the 1990s that the real growth in CCTV occurred.

The last Conservative government saw crime start to soar dramatically. From 1982 to 1992, crime had risen by 74 per cent in England and Wales, and the number of crimes detected by the police had fallen from 37 to 26 per cent. The Audit Commission conducted a review, which looked at the effectiveness of crime management within the police service. The report identified three main areas that should be tackled:

- developing strategies to clarify roles and accountabilities;

- making the best use of resources;

- targeting criminals rather than responding to crime incidents.

The report criticised the ability of the police to reduce and detect crime, and made a number of recommendations to improve performance. It highlighted the key role of crime prevention, together with the expansion of proactive and intelligence-led policing. The use of CCTV as an effective crime prevention measure was highlighted, and the report provided examples of success in Airdrie town centre and in sheltered accommodation in Merseyside (Home Office, 1993).

It was apparent at this time that there was much political support for the development of CCTV schemes, and there was also good evidence of public support. One incident that really brought the use of CCTV to the fore was the tragic murder of two-year-old James Bulger in February1993. James was abducted by two ten-year-old boys in the Bootle Strand shopping centre, Liverpool, and led away to a place where he was tortured and murdered. CCTV footage was broadcast nationally and showed James walking out of the shopping centre with his killers. This image was dramatically etched on to the minds of the general public and launched the debate about the use of CCTV as a legitimate and necessary means of crime control that could make a real contribution to community safety and in reducing the fear of crime.

Government support

In October 1994, the then Home Secretary, Michael Howard, announced a City Challenge competition, supported with £2 million funding, to develop CCTV schemes. The response was overwhelming, with 480 bids received, and the fund was increased by a further £5 million, which was only sufficient for 106 of the bids made. The conditions of the challenge were that each bidder had to find partnership funding, for example from local businesses, police, local authorities and other government departments, and would also be responsible for any running costs. Such was the success of the scheme that the government provided further funding, which had risen to £37 million by 1997 (Norris and Armstrong, 1999, p36).

New Labour, on taking power in 1997, continued with the City Challenge competition, but only added a further £1 million for the development of CCTV schemes. In 1999, the government published an ambitious crime reduction programme and announced that it was to continue with the expansion of CCTV, providing a further £153 million for its development over a three-year period. In the decade 1992–2002, the government invested nearly a quarter of a billion pounds of public money in developing national CCTV schemes. This, however, was only a small proportion of the overall investment when added to the money provided by partner organisations (Norris, 2003, p255).

National CCTV Strategy

In October 2007, the government introduced its latest *National CCTV Strategy*, written in conjunction with ACPO. Tony McNulty (Secretary of State for Security) states in his foreword:

> *The United Kingdom is generally recognised as a leading user of Closed Circuit Television (CCTV) for community safety and crime investigation purposes . . . I see CCTV as an important tool in the Government's crime-fighting strategy.*
>
> (Home Office, 2007, p4)

The report claims that the UK enjoys significant public support and that crime surveys provide evidence that the public feel safer as a result of CCTV; however, the report recognises that the development of CCTV systems has been piecemeal, with little strategic direction, control or regulation. Opportunities have been missed to maximise fully the potential of the technology and problems have been identified, such as the move from video to digital evidence, lack of a coordinated approach to CCTV development with risks to the compatibility of systems, the cost of processing images, and the loss of operational effectiveness.

The strategy provides 44 recommendations to be tackled by all agencies responsible for CCTV and a multi-agency programme board has been put in place to implement the recommendations made. The report (Home Office, 2007, p5) identifies the issues as fitting into ten broad groups:

- national standards for all aspects of CCTV;

- clear guidelines for registration, inspection and enforcement;

- training of personnel;

- police use of CCTV footage and evidence;

- issues relating to storage, volume, archiving and retention;

- development of CCTV networks;

- equipping, resourcing and standardisation in the CJS;

- emerging technologies, changing threats and new/changing priorities;

- partnership working;

- financial and resource management.

The government clearly sees the use of CCTV technology as being a main strand of its strategy to tackle the problems of crime and disorder effectively, to improve public confidence in the CJS, and to contribute significantly to community safety. We shall discuss later in this chapter whether this is the case, or if we are developing a surveillance society that is slowly eroding precious human rights.

PRACTICAL TASK

- *Have you ever considered the fact that you are being watched and monitored on a regular basis? Think about a day in your life and list all of the potential places where you might be filmed while going about your daily business.*

- *Write down how you personally feel about being watched by CCTV and make a list of what you consider to be the benefits and the disadvantages of the use of CCTV as part of a community safety strategy.*

Key legislation

This section examines the following Acts of Parliament that relate directly to the management and use of CCTV evidence within the CJS:

- Criminal Justice and Public Order Act (CJPOA) 1994;

- Criminal Procedures and Investigations Act (CPIA) 1996;

- Human Rights Act (HRA) 1998;

- Data Protection Act (DPA) 1998;

- Freedom of Information Act (FOIA) 2000;

- Regulation of Investigatory Powers Act (RIPA) 2000.

Criminal Justice and Public Order Act 1994

Section 163 of this Act allows a local authority, in consultation with the Chief Police Officer, to provide or arrange for the provision of CCTV within its area with the purpose of promoting the prevention of crime and the welfare of victims of crime.

Criminal Procedure and Investigations Act 1996

This Act followed a recommendation made by Viscount Runciman of Doxford, who chaired a Royal Commission on Criminal Justice in 1993. It introduced for the first time the concept of disclosure – the requirement for the prosecution to disclose all material gathered during the course of a criminal investigation. The rules are designed to ensure that the accused is provided with a fair trial.

An investigator has a duty to record and retain all material that is gathered during a criminal investigation. CCTV recordings or digital images are material for the purposes of the Act and, when available to an investigator, should be seized, recorded, retained and revealed to the defence. Material that is not required as part of the prosecution case is listed as 'unused material' and is disclosed to the defence, except for material that is classified as 'sensitive'. Sensitive material is material that the investigator believes it is not in the public interest to disclose, although the approval of a court may be required at a public interest immunity hearing.

Deletion of, or failure to seize and retain, any relevant CCTV recordings or digital images during the course of an investigation may be in breach of the Act if they are not available for later disclosure. It may provide the defence with grounds to challenge the fairness of the trial because of the unavailability of the evidence.

CASE STUDY

The following two cases provide examples of where a conviction has been challenged when CCTV evidence has not been seized or retained.

R (Ebrahim) v. Feltham Magistrates Court [2001]
This case concerned a charge of common assault in a superstore. The investigating officer had viewed the store's CCTV footage and found no evidence in relation to the allegation of assault and, as a result, did not seize the videotape, which was reused by the store some weeks later. The defendant argued that the videotape was essential to his defence, and because it had been destroyed he could not have a fair trial.

Mouat v. Director of Public Prosecutions [2001]
The police had stopped a driver for speeding and issued him with a fixed penalty notice. The defendant was asked to sit in the police car, where he was shown video footage of

---

the speeding offence. The police did not retain the video evidence because the excessive speed was recorded on an internal speeding device within the police vehicle, and the videotape was recycled some weeks later. The defendant argued that there was an abuse of the process of the court on the grounds that the videotape was essential to his defence, and because it had been destroyed he could not have a fair trial.

These cases were considered together by the appeal court, which considered previous court decisions relating to similar cases and reviewed the requirements of the CPIA, together with the guidance found in associated codes of practice. The court recognised the need to establish the extent of the duty for the prosecution to obtain, or retain in its possession, the videotaped material and that, where a duty did exist, the defendant could, on the balance of probabilities, show that it was no longer possible to conduct a fair trial.

REFLECTIVE TASK

Access Westlaw or Lexis Library online and find the two cases highlighted above. Read through the appeal court judgment and find the references made to the CPIA and its associated codes of practice. Reflect on how they have been applied in the decision-making process of the court and what the implications are for criminal investigators.

Human Rights Act 1998

The HRA was first introduced in 2000 and sets out a number of basic human rights that need to be respected by a public authority (which includes government, police, local authority, courts, etc.). The Act reflects the European Convention on Human Rights, signed by the UK in 1951, and citizens are now able to challenge any breach of the rights set out within the Act through a UK court.

In respect of CCTV and the monitoring of persons in a public space, there are rights that need to be respected by a public authority when considering policy and procedures of operation:

- article 6 – right to a fair trial;
- article 8 – right to respect for private and family life.

Right to a fair trial

How CCTV images are captured, retrieved, copied, handled and stored by both the police and third parties is critical to ensure the integrity of any evidence relied upon in a criminal prosecution. Lawyers scrutinise any evidence produced and want to ensure that relevant legislation and codes of practice have been adhered to. Legislation and codes of practice provide safeguards for those responsible for managing and maintaining a CCTV system and for the investigator whose role it is to secure and obtain evidence. For example, full audit trails will be required for any CCTV image obtained in order to prove continuity of the evidence, including the copying and editing process, how the image has been stored, and how it has been handled.

Right to respect for private and family life

This right imposes a positive obligation on the State to ensure that its laws provide adequate protection against the unjustified disclosure of personal data. The provision or release of personal data without consent, and the collection and storage of personal data without consent, are construed as interference with an individual's right to respect for his or her privacy. As we shall see in the next section relating to the DPA, a CCTV image can be classified as 'personal data' and is subject to privacy laws.

It has been established in law that a CCTV recording of an individual in a public place may, in certain circumstances, be regarded as the recording of a private situation (*Peck* v. *UK* [2003]). The HRA provides for a number of circumstances where it is justified to interfere with the privacy of an individual, for example a digital recording of an individual in a public space that is required for evidential purposes by the police. The Act provides that the owner of the data (public authority) and the police must be able to show that their actions were legal, necessary and proportionate, in that:

- there is a legal authority that allows the sharing of the data, for example the DPA provides the lawful authority for processing private data;

- it is necessary in a democratic society, in the interests of national security, public safety or the economic well-being of the country, for the prevention of disorder or crime, for the protection of health or morals, or for the protection of the rights and freedoms of others;

- the action taken is proportionate, for example there may be less intrusive means of obtaining the evidence required for a criminal conviction.

Data Protection Act 1998

The DPA gives individuals the right to access any personal data held by any organisation about them and also sets out how organisations should process and use the data, including how they are acquired, stored, shared and disposed of. The government has appointed an Information Commissioner, whose responsibility it is to enforce the provisions of the Act following any contraventions of it.

'Personal data' are defined as anything that relates to a living individual who can be identified from that data (s1(1)), and includes a CCTV recording or digital image. The Act also provides a definition of 'sensitive personal data', to which additional rules apply as to their data processing and use.

Schedule 1 of the DPA sets out eight key principles relating to personal data.

1. They shall be processed fairly and lawfully.

2. They shall be obtained only for a lawful purpose and processed only in accordance with the lawful purpose.

3. They shall be adequate, relevant and not excessive for the purpose for which they are processed.

4. They shall be accurate and kept up to date.

5. They shall not be kept for longer than necessary.

6. They shall be processed in accordance with individuals' rights.

7. Appropriate technical and organisational measures shall be taken against unauthorised or unlawful processing, and against accidental loss or destruction of, or damage to, personal data.

8. They shall not be transferred to another country or territory outside the European Economic Area without adequate protection.

There may be certain circumstances when the DPA does not apply to a CCTV recording or digital image, such as an automatic system that does not focus on individuals. It would only apply if an attempt was later made to identify the individual by using other data to cross-reference that on the recording or digital image. Where the CCTV system is used primarily to identify individuals or criminal activity, the Act would apply, for example in town centres, shopping malls and railway stations.

The general rule is that any personal data should remain confidential, but the DPA provides a number of exceptions to this rule, which include national security (s28); the prevention and detection of crime (s29(a)); and the apprehension or prosecution of offenders (s29(b)).

Freedom of Information Act 2000

This Act provides the opportunity for any member of the public to make an application to access information that is held by a public authority. This applies to all kinds of information, including a CCTV recording or digital image, but does not include personal data and sensitive personal data, such as racial or ethnic origin, sexual life, political opinions or religious beliefs (see section 2 of the DPA). A public authority is required to produce and maintain a publication scheme that sets out the type of information that will be provided by them on request. When a request is made for information, the public authority is required to respond, confirming that it has the information requested, and then supply it within 20 working days.

The Act sets out a number of exemptions that allow a public authority to refuse to provide the information requested. Some of these exemptions that the police service relies on include those relating to national security (s24); criminal investigations and proceedings (s30); and law enforcement (s31). This assists the police in being able to protect information that, if released, would be prejudicial to carrying out their core roles of law enforcement, crime prevention and the protection of life.

Go to the website of the Information Commissioner's Office at www.ico.gov.uk and access the link on the menu 'Tools and Resources'. Then access the link 'Decision Notices' and insert the following information into the search fields: Case ref. number (FS50066908) and date (April 2006). The search will provide you with access to an appeal relating to the Bristol North Primary Care Trust, which refused to provide a copy of a CCTV recording to a member of the public whose car had been damaged in a hospital car park.

Read through the decision made by the Information Commissioner and see how the law has been applied. This will provide you with a good example of the application of the HRA, DPA and FOIA.

The Regulation of Investigatory Powers Act 2000

This chapter is concerned with overt rather than covert use of CCTV; however, it is appropriate to mention the implications of this Act when a public CCTV system is used for a specific investigation or operation in which covert surveillance may be necessary.

Covert surveillance is defined as any surveillance that is carried out in a manner calculated to ensure that the persons subject to the surveillance are unaware that it is or may be taking place (s26(9)(a)). The Act states that covert surveillance can be directed or intrusive and, in both cases, authorisation is required before the surveillance can be carried out. Without authorisation the surveillance is deemed to be unlawful and any evidence obtained is likely to be excluded by a court.

When a CCTV system is used for covert surveillance, an application is made to a person who can authorise the surveillance. Within the police service this person may be an Inspector or Superintendent who, before granting any authorisation, will consider all aspects of the application, including issues of legality, necessity and proportionality. The application will be set out in writing, together with the decision made, and will be subject to the laws of disclosure.

House of Lords Select Committee on the Constitution

In February 2009, a House of Lords Select Committee published a report entitled *Surveillance: Citizens and the State*, following enquiries made about 'The impact that government surveillance and data collection have upon the privacy of citizens and their relationship with the State' (House of Lords, 2009, p6).

The report raises a series of issues relating to the broader picture of the use of surveillance within the UK, including the development and use of CCTV surveillance. A series of recommendations have been made with two relating directly to CCTV surveillance. The first asks for an independent review of research evidence on the effectiveness of CCTV in preventing, detecting and investigating crime (paragraph 468). The second relates directly to legislative control and recommends that a statutory regime should be introduced by government for both public and private sector CCTV operators, supported by codes of practice legally binding on all CCTV schemes, with a further system for complaints and remedies (paragraph 469). It is likely that we will see the introduction of new legislation relating to the use of CCTV surveillance in the near future.

PRACTICAL TASK

Go to www.parliament.uk – enter Surveillance: Citizens and the State *in the search field at the top of the web page and find chapter 4, 'Regulation of CCTV', paragraphs 213–19).*

Read through this section of the report, which makes the recommendation for more regulation of CCTV in both public and private sectors. Make a note of what key organisations have to say and consider whether there is a pressing need for more regulation today. Make a list of the advantages and disadvantages of additional legislation.

CCTV Code of Practice

A *Code of Practice* for operators of CCTV systems is currently available and was revised by the Information Commissioner in 2008. A code of practice provides guidance that should be followed to ensure good practice standards and to operate within the law. Any breach of the code may render any evidence obtained inadmissible in a court of law in certain circumstances, or may leave the operator or investigator open to civil litigation. Further, if the code is not adhered to, public confidence and support may be lost.

Most CCTV systems used by organisations or businesses are designed to view and record the activities of individuals and will be subject to the DPA. The code ensures that those responsible for capturing images of individuals comply with the DPA and reassure those whose images are captured, and also that the images captured are usable. The code is applicable to users of CCTV who capture images of individuals for the purposes of seeing what an individual is doing, for example monitoring in a shop or walking down the street; taking some action in relation to the individual, such as handing images over to the police; or using images of an individual that impact on their privacy, such as providing images to the media.

The code provides guidance for compliance by both large and small-scale users of CCTV systems. The following (adapted from Information Commissioner, 2008, p21) is a checklist of items covered by the code that relate to the small-scale user, such as a shop retailer, who needs to ensure that:

- a named controller is identified who is responsible for the CCTV equipment and recordings;

- notification is provided to the Information Commissioner about the CCTV system and its use;

- the system is required specifically for the prevention and detection of crime, and for protecting the safety of customers, and is not to be used for any other purpose;

- cameras are sited so that the images are clear enough for any police investigation;

- cameras are positioned so as not to view persons not visiting the premises;

- signs are displayed stating that cameras are in operation and identifying the name of the controller or other responsible person;

- images from the camera are stored securely and with limited access;

- images are retained for a period long enough only for any incident to come to light;

- recordings are only made available to law enforcement agencies and not to third parties;

- the system is regularly checked to ensure that it is working properly;

- the controller knows how to respond to individuals making requests for copies of their own images, or how to seek advice from the Information Commissioner following a request.

PRACTICAL TASK

Go to www.ico.gov.uk/for_organisations/topic_specific_guides/cctv.aspx to view the CCTV Code of Practice: Revised edition 2008. *As part of your research, you may wish to see the code being applied in practice, so if an opportunity is available consider a visit to a local operator to see the code working in practice.*

(Note: some caution may be necessary as there will be restricted access to some CCTV centres and some operators may be reluctant to assist due to business demands or their non-compliance with code. If you are not sure, seek advice from an appropriate person, such as a supervisor or lecturer.)

Retrieval of video and CCTV evidence

It is recognised good practice for the police service to keep records of all CCTV systems being operated in both public and private locations, such as police/local authority monitoring centres, the road system, car parks, hospitals, public houses, sporting venues, public buildings and retail premises. CCTV images can provide useful evidence for crime investigators, tracing witnesses to a crime, or assisting in locating an offender who has made off from the scene of a crime. They can also have non-crime uses, such as locating a missing person or identifying safety hazards.

Recordings of images can be captured in various formats, such as videotape, CD, DVD or extracts from computerised systems. When it is known that images are available and relevant to a criminal investigation, they should be seized as soon as possible before any evidence is lost. When the evidence is seized, it should be sealed and securely stored with an exhibit label attached. Full written records are required to ensure both the evidential integrity and the continuity of the exhibit.

A copy of the recording will need to be made (working copy), should the recording be required for further investigative work. The police service must adhere to local instructions before any copying takes place, as there may be circumstances where the evidence could be corrupted or lost, or where specialist advice and equipment are needed to make the copy.

For some of the more serious crime investigations, it may not be possible to view immediately all of the potential CCTV evidence available, but it will be essential to seize as much as possible for later viewing. A Senior Investigating Officer (SIO) is usually responsible for providing parameters to investigators tasked with seizing CCTV evidence.

PRACTICAL TASK

A serious assault has occurred outside a nightclub in the town centre one evening, and the offender has made off on foot. A witness claims that the offender had a vehicle parked nearby.

Make a list of potential sources of CCTV evidence and consider how it may assist an investigation.

You may have recognised the potential of a CCTV system to capture images of the incident, assist in identifying the offender, provide the identity of potential witnesses, and identify the vehicle used by the offender to escape.

Digital CCTV evidence

In 2007, ACPO published guidance for the retrieval of digital CCTV evidence. Digital CCTV technology is developing at a rapid rate, providing new challenges for investigators to secure and process captured images effectively for evidential purposes that often require specialist knowledge or equipment.

The guidance advises that, when CCTV images are to be retrieved by a police officer from third parties, such as CCTV schemes or retailers, it is preferable that the images be downloaded by the system owner or administrator and then given to the officer. If the officer is required to retrieve the images, local procedures should be adhered to or specialist advice sought where appropriate. Where the capture system presents significant difficulties, a specialist should be deployed to facilitate the retrieval of the images. Once the image has been secured, it is imperative that an audit trail is started (ACPO, 2007, p14).

A full audit trail is required from the point of image capture, or at the point of retrieval or seizure if generated by a third party. The audit trail will document all the working processes, from the initial master copy (original) to the working copy and to the end product, such as an enhanced image used to identify a suspect. This is essential for compliance with the rules of disclosure, and to ensure the integrity of the evidence (ACPO, 2007, p25).

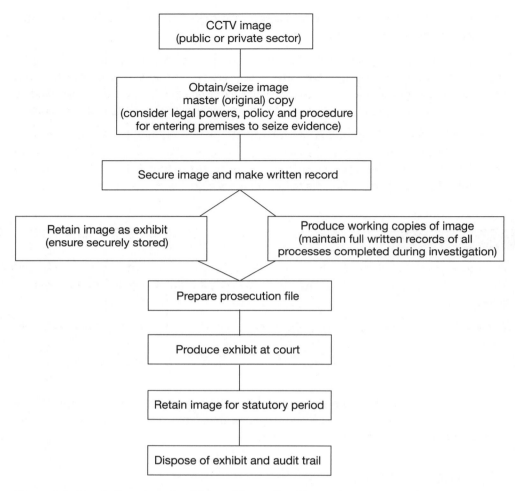

Figure 6.1 Simple flowchart for CCTV evidence (local procedures may vary)

Evaluation of CCTV surveillance

The Home Office has completed a number of evaluations since the introduction of CCTV surveillance as a crime prevention measure and this section will provide an overview of some of the findings from the evaluations.

CCTV in Town Centres

In 1995, it was recognised that nearly half of all councils had installed CCTV within their town centres. Little evaluation had taken place in respect of the impact of CCTV and there was a growing concern from both the public and private retailers, who were seeking reassurance that the investment made was having an impact on crime control.

The aim of the research (Home Office, 1995) was to examine how the police use CCTV systems to tackle crime and disorder within a town centre, and how the systems impact on the overall crime rate. The three towns concerned were Newcastle, Birmingham and King's Lynn, and the methodology included interviews with key personnel and examination of data.

The findings of the evaluation can be summarised as follows.

- There was a strong deterrent factor short term, but deterrent could wane longer term if not used to increase the risk of arrest for certain offences.

- Property crime was reduced, especially burglary, with no evidence of displacement of the crime elsewhere.

- There was a limited effect on personal crimes such as assault, but it prompted many arrests; however, it was recognised that it facilitated quicker responses that could reduce the seriousness of an incident.

- Information could save police resources by preventing false alarms.

- There was a reduction in costs for investigation and prosecution; it provided assistance in directing investigations and obtaining swifter convictions.

- Birmingham saw a reduction in robbery and theft from the person, but displacement of the crime was evident in areas not covered by CCTV.

- People who were aware of the cameras felt safer on the street at night.

Crime Prevention Effects of Closed Circuit Television

This report (Home Office, 2002) summarised the findings of a number of previous studies from both the UK and USA that investigated the effectiveness of CCTV in crime prevention. It drew conclusions on the effectiveness of CCTV generally, and its effectiveness in specific settings, such as car parks, public transport and city centres.

The research found that CCTV had little impact on violent crime, but did have a significant effect on vehicle crime when utilised in car parks. However, it recognised that other interventions, such as camera notices or improved lighting, contributed to the reductions seen.

The government's heavy investment in developing CCTV systems at the time of the report is highlighted. It is identified as the single most heavily funded non-criminal justice crime prevention measure, with three-quarters of the total crime prevention budget being spent on CCTV development during the period 1996–98.

The report concludes by stating that CCTV reduces crime to a small degree and suggests that future CCTV schemes should be carefully implemented and fully evaluated, and that attempts should be made to identify how CCTV impacts on crime.

National Evaluation of CCTV

As mentioned earlier, the CCTV initiative was introduced by the Labour government in 1999 as part of their crime reduction strategy and its aims were threefold:

- to assist local crime and disorder reduction partnerships to deploy CCTV in areas identified by local crime audits as having significant crime and disorder problems;

- to develop the knowledge base of how CCTV can most effectively contribute to reducing crime and disorder;

- to support delivery of local crime reduction strategies with the aim of reducing crime and disorder, and specifically of reducing vehicle crime by 30 per cent.

The report (Home Office, 2003) examined the lessons learnt from the setting up of 17 CCTV schemes that had been funded by the government initiative, and identified seven key aspects to assist practitioners in the setting up of future schemes: the pre-bidding process, project management, building a project team, engagement of stakeholders, third parties, identification of costs and resources, and design and technology.

Assessing the Impact of CCTV

This research (Home Office, 2005) was based on 13 CCTV projects funded in phase two of the government's CCTV initiative, and it examined the use of CCTV in different locations, including city and town centres, car parks, hospitals and residential areas. The research was designed to explore a number of different aspects by examining:

- crime patterns to identify changes in levels of crime and any displacement of crime to other areas;

- public attitude surveys to assess changes in public perceptions of CCTV;

- other crime prevention initiatives that could have an impact on changes in crime patterns;

- the process of choosing CCTV as an option and how it is evaluated as providing the best option to tackle local crime and disorder problems;

- technical specifications and design, and how CCTV should be implemented and installed;

- control room operations and management, and working relationships with key players such as the police;

- the economic impact of each system.

REFLECTIVE TASK

Go to www.homeoffice.gov.uk/rds/pdfs05/hors292.pdf and download the 2005 report discussed in the last section. Chapter 2 will provide you with an overview of the CCTV schemes evaluated during the research.

Read the concluding section (pages 115–21) and consider the arguments presented about the effectiveness of CCTV as a viable crime prevention strategy. Compare and contrast the negative and positive aspects of the report with previous findings.

You will have found that some of the comments made appear to be quite damning, such as:

> *Assessed on the evidence presented in this report, CCTV cannot be deemed a success. It has cost a lot of money and it has not produced the anticipated benefits.*

> (Home Office, 2005, p120)

However, attempts have been made to highlight the positive elements of CCTV and you will note that a number of observations have been made to assist policy makers, CCTV operators and managers in making the best use of CCTV technology and in maximising its potential as part of a viable crime reduction and community safety strategy.

Surveillance society and the spectre of 'Big Brother'

There is no doubt that the use of CCTV within our society continues to grow at an alarming rate, suggested by some commentators as being unchecked and unregulated. The sophistication of CCTV technology is also developing at a rapid rate, with face recognition systems, smart CCTV that can detect behavioural patterns, audio links (talking lamp-posts), and reading of registration numbers on both roads and car parks for traffic regulation.

George Orwell, in his infamous novel *1984*, provided a picture of a totalitarian state with its citizens' every move being monitored. Civil liberty groups have warned about the erosion of privacy (Crossman et al., 2007) and some are questioning whether this fiction is becoming a reality:

> *The Big Brother nightmare of George Orwell's 1984 has become a reality – in the shadow of the author's former London home. It may have taken a little longer than he predicted, but Orwell's vision of a society where cameras and computers spy on every person's movements is now here.*

> (*London Evening News*, 2007)

The State has a clear mandate to protect its citizens, but must balance this duty against an individual's right to privacy. The House of Lords Select Committee report, *Surveillance: Citizens and the State*, makes a clear recommendation for further independent research (see page 92 of this book). It recognised that the use of CCTV is popular with law-abiding people, but that research tends to suggest that its impact on preventing crime is limited. ACPO sees CCTV as a vital element of crime investigation, and the arrest and conviction in 2000 of the London nail bomber, David Copeland, provides a good example of the effectiveness of CCTV. Transport for London has over 10,000 cameras, which are used for system management, and for delivering a safe and secure environment. These cameras provided key evidence for the investigations into the terrorist bombings in July 2005 (House of Lords, 2009, p22).

In contrast, in January 2010 the media reported that CCTV cameras were being used to issue 'ghost' parking tickets, generating up to £3 million a year in fines – a trend that other councils are expected to follow (Warren, 2010).

REFLECTIVE TASK

Consider the proposition that CCTV is contributing to us all now living in a surveillance state, where privacy is a thing of the past. Develop an argument in support of, or against, the proposition made, outlining both the benefits and disadvantages of CCTV technology.

C H A P T E R   S U M M A R Y

This chapter has provided a historical perspective of the development and growth of CCTV systems in the UK. Government responses and interventions have been explored, including key legislation, national policy, and academic evaluation of the approach. Opportunities have been provided for further research, and analysis of certain issues relating to CCTV surveillance will provide stimulus, sources and evidence for completion of NOS and assignments. Further academic reading and research will provide a more detailed understanding of the use of CCTV in contemporary investigation and its impact on both the individual and the State.

REFERENCES

Association of Chief Police Officers (ACPO) (2007) *Practice Advice on Police Use of Digital Images*. Wyboston: National Policing Improvement Agency.

Crossman, Gareth, with Kitchin, Hilary, Kuna, Rekha, Skrein, Michael and Russell, Jago (2007) *Overlooked: Surveillance and personal privacy in modern Britain*. London: Liberty/The Nuffield Foundation.

Home Office (1993) *Helping with Enquiries: Tackling crime effectively*, Audit Commission Report. London: HMSO/College Hill Press.

Home Office (1995) *CCTV in Town Centres: Three case studies*. London: Police Research Group.

Home Office (2002) *Crime Prevention Effects of Closed Circuit Television: A systematic review*. London: RDS.

Home Office (2003) *National Evaluation of CCTV: Early findings on scheme implementation – effective practice guide*. London: RDS.

Home Office (2005) *Assessing the Impact of CCTV*. London: RDS.

Home Office (2007) *National CCTV Strategy: October 2007*. London: Association of Chief Police Officers.

House of Lords (2009) *Surveillance: Citizens and the State – Volume 1: Report*. London: The Stationery Office.

Information Commissioner (2008) *CCTV Code of Practice*, revised edition. Wilmslow: Information Commissioner's Office.

Information Commissioner (2009) *CCTV*. Available online at www.ico.gov.uk/for_organisations/topic_specific_guides/cctv.aspx (accessed 7 April 2009).

London Evening News (2007) George Orwell, Big Brother is watching your house. *London Evening News*, 31 March. Available online at www.thisislondon.co.uk/news/article-23391081-details/ George+Orwell,+Big+Brother+is+watching+your+house/article.do (accessed 30 April 2009).

Norris, Clive (2003) From personal to digital, in Lyon, David (ed.) *Surveillance as Social Sorting: Privacy, risk and digital discrimination*. London: Routledge.

Norris, Clive and Armstrong, Gary (1999) *The Maximum Surveillance Society: The rise of CCTV*. Oxford: Berg.

Warren, Scott (2010) Councils use CCTV to collect £3 million in 'ghost' parking tickets every year. *The Daily Mail*, 12 January. Available online at www.dailymail.co.uk/news/article-1242513/CCTV-cameras-collecting-3million-year-ghost-parking-tickets.html (accessed 13 January 2010).

USEFUL WEBSITES

www.cctv-information.co.uk (CCTV information from the CCTV Advisory Service)

www.cctvusergroup.com (CCTV User Group)

www.crimereduction.homeoffice.gov.uk/cctv (The National CCTV Strategy website)

www.ico.gov.uk (Information Commissioner's Office, which has links to the Data Protection Act and how to request CCTV footage under this Act)

www.parliament.co.uk (UK Parliament website, which has links to legislation)

www.surveillance-and-society.org (*Surveillance & Society* is an online journal covering varied aspects of surveillance and its impact)

CASES

Mouat v. *Director of Public Prosecutions* [2001] EWCH Admin 130

Peck v. *United Kingdom* [2003] European Court of Human Rights 36 EHRR 41:57

R (Ebrahim) v. *Feltham Magistrates' Court* [2001] 1 WLR 1293

LEGISLATION

Criminal Justice and Public Order Act 1994

Criminal Procedures and Investigations Act 1996

Data Protection Act 1998

Freedom of Information Act 2000

Human Rights Act 1998

Regulation of Investigatory Powers Act 2000

7 Counterfeiting: the part technology and the Internet play

Introduction

In this chapter we are going to look at the offence of counterfeiting and concentrate on the investigative process both from the intelligence and evidential point of view.

Intellectual property (IP) crime is a general phrase used to describe a number of counterfeiting and piracy offences, and intellectual property rights (IPR) are temporary grants of control intended to give economic incentives for innovative work. IPR exist in the form of patents, copyrights, trade secrets and trademarks. The private sector is now investing more and more in product protection, and in the proactive auditing of IPR data in order to identify evidence of theft.

These offences also include the counterfeiting of banknotes and pharmaceuticals. These are serious crimes that defraud and threaten the well-being of the public, and some even pose a significant safety threat on a global scale. This takes place when innocent customers and sick patients put their health, and even their lives, at risk when they use counterfeit pharmaceuticals that contain little or no active (main) ingredients.

There is general agreement that IP crime is high-profit and low-risk, which predictably motivates individuals to engage in this type of activity in order to fund their criminality (Interpol, 2010).

Counterfeiting, copyright and trademark infringements

The Federation Against Copyright Theft (FACT) is the UK's lead agency in this field and its main purpose is to protect the country's film and broadcasting industry against such infringements. It was established in 1983 and works in three crucial areas:

- online piracy in all forms – with a focus on those distributing large volumes of illicit film and television content;

- hard goods piracy – organised criminal networks operating in the UK (and worldwide) have adopted audio-visual piracy as a crime type to generate substantial illegal profits;

- prevention and detection of illegal recording in cinemas – over 90 per cent of the counterfeit versions of movies originate initially from a copy recorded in a cinema.

According to FACT, the film piracy business in the UK generates £200 million a year for the criminal fraternity. However, through their technical and forensic capabilities, FACT continues to support law enforcement agencies to increase the number of investigations of the main players involved and to restrict, reduce and eventually close down their commercial and distribution networks (FACT, 2010).

PRACTICAL TASK

Read thorough the various investigative case summaries in relation to the selling and production of counterfeit music and films, which can be found at www.fact-uk.org.uk/site/latest_news/index.htm.

Identify how technology and the Internet were used to facilitate the crimes, and how much profit was being made by those involved.

Counterfeit currency

The crime of counterfeiting banknotes can undermine the economic stability of a nation and inflict serious financial losses on the public. The continued improvement of photographic and computer technology, as well as printing devices, has made the production of counterfeit currency somewhat easy.

There are three key methods that can be intermixed to create counterfeit banknotes. The selection of method(s) used will be based on how good the counterfeiter wants the final note to be, what sort of amount is required, the time available, the skills of those involved and the accessibility and availability of the right equipment.

The first method is to use a computer-based scanner and printer system, or a colour copier connected to such a system. The second method is when traditional lithographic printing is used to reproduce the artwork, along with various techniques to replicate any additional security features such as watermarks. The third method is to use computer-generated artwork and prepare the plates in a conventional way.

The first method is the easiest, most costly and very time-intensive if those involved are attempting to produce large numbers of counterfeit notes. The second method is the most difficult, but it does give the best results. The third method is the traditional compromise, as it is reasonably straightforward with the right equipment, and produces a fairly high-quality counterfeit note.

Characteristically, over 90 per cent of all counterfeit banknotes have been produced using the last method. However, because of the developments in new technology and the ease of access to it, from 2000 there was a significant move towards involving computers. This was evidenced at the time by the arrest and conviction of two very active counterfeiters.

CASE STUDY

Anthony Grimes and Paul Jones

On the 23 April 2001, Anthony Grimes was jailed for his leading role in producing £10 million in counterfeit currency. Grimes, who had worked in the print business, also made fake passports and motoring documents for organised crime. His criminal associate and fellow printer, Paul Jones, brought with him essential computer skills that allowed this criminal endeavour to become more streamlined and more efficient. Out went some of the noisy and unwieldy printing machinery and in came modern technology. This development meant not only changes in the means of production but also an overall improvement in product quality, which resulted in them being the first counterfeiters to forge the Bank of England's new £20 note, which included a complex hologram.

In sentencing Grimes to seven and a half years' imprisonment and Jones to five years' imprisonment, His Honour Judge Stewart stated:

> *You [Jones] brought to the scheme your skills in the use of computers. You went about obtaining the appropriate equipment and your involvement was taking this conspiracy onto a higher plane, both in terms of the finished product and no doubt in terms of the potential gains.*

> *(Regina v. Grimes and Jones [2001])*

Stephen Jory

In the early 1990s, there was an unprecedented increase in the amount of counterfeit currency circulating throughout the UK. The rise occurred across the board in both sterling and foreign banknotes, and reached a peak in 2002 (Bank of England, 2009).

To combat this, law enforcement began a proactive operation involving Stephen Jory, with a view to identifying printing premises and the main criminals around him. Jory had been the subject of previous operations and had become aware of covert and technical policing methods, as a result of which he proved to be an extremely difficult target to tackle and, therefore, even more difficult to convict.

On Monday, 19 December 1994, cuttings of paper were found protruding from and in front of a garage rented by Jory in the name Stephen James. These cuttings proved to be from the edge of sheets of counterfeit £20 notes. The next day, Jory entered the garage and was about to get into a motor vehicle parked within when he was joined by officers from the then South East Regional Crime Squad (SERCS).

The subsequent search revealed a large quantity of completed counterfeit £20 notes, with the indicative reference E/20/12 (see below). They also found rolls of foils used to make the metal strip in counterfeit notes and 17 metal plates, each plate having a different part of the £20 note impregnated on it. The plates together would give a person the capability to print counterfeit £20 notes.

Jory was released from prison and went back to what he knew best – counterfeiting. However, he was caught again in August 1998 when attempting to hand over to another criminal two holdalls stuffed with counterfeit £20 notes that had a face value of £750,000. The subsequent police action led to a number of search warrants being executed, one of which was for the home address of Kenneth Mainstone. In a building next to the main house was a large print shop that contained a four-colour lithographic printer, a plate maker, a guillotine and printing blankets bearing images of the Queen's head (Regina v. Jory, Mainstone and others [1999]).

> *Jory and his accomplices had already flooded Britain with fakes when in 1998 the police caught the gang whom they had nicknamed the 'Lavender Hill Mob'. Although Jory admitted to a charge of having produced £50m-worth of counterfeit £20 notes, the real figure is probably much higher – his notes were so convincing that they fooled UV counterfeit detectors and in some places were redistributed through the banking system. After his incarceration, the Bank of England was forced to change the design of the £20 note in order to add extra security features.*
>
> *(Willis, 2006)*

In the first case, Jory received 21 months' imprisonment and, in the second, eight years' imprisonment – he spent his fiftieth birthday in prison.

Classification of counterfeit currency

The Bank of England classifies all counterfeit notes with an indicative reference, for example 'E/20/12'. The initial letter E refers to the fact that it is a reproduction of a series E note. The number 20 refers to the fact that is a £20 note. The number 12 refers to the fact that it is the twelfth series of printed counterfeits of this note.

A second example would be 'E/20/CC'. This refers to colour-, laser- or inkjet-printed counterfeits. Copies of this type are not separately identified because almost every one seized is different.

PRACTICAL TASK

Access the article, 'Counterfeit Bank of England banknotes', at www.bankofengland. co.uk/banknotes/about/counterfeits.htm.

Work your way through the article and discover the facts and figures surrounding the seizure of counterfeit currency between 2002 and 2009, what legislation is used to deal with this type of crime, and how the Bank of England combats the production and distribution of counterfeit currency through the use of technology.

Counterfeiting investigative strategies

Modern technology was at the heart of the investigative differences between the Grimes and Jory investigations (see Case study above); in part, a computer file replaced the traditional method of making a printing plate. Such digital files can be encrypted, duplicated or even stored on an overseas computer, making it much more difficult for investigators to discover, and even harder to take possession of. Computer files are also easy to pass on, whether in the pub or over the Internet. It is therefore feasible for an individual or group to store a collection of high-quality images of banknotes from around the world in a secure and inaccessible location.

The Grimes and Jory investigations were successful as a result of one or more of the following investigative techniques.

- Various methods of 'real-world' and technical intelligence-gathering led to the breaking of coded messages between those involved.

- Counterfeit distribution was analysed through the use of indicatives and the price an individual pays for a counterfeit. As with any form of commerce, the price goes up as the product is sold on from the manufacturer to others in the chain of distribution.

- To combat surveillance-savvy criminals, staggered and technical surveillance was employed. This is where you follow an individual from point A to B, then the next time you wait for them to come to point B and follow them to point C, and so on.

- 'Real-world' and technical subterfuge was used to obtain details of associates.

- There was innovative and methodical forensic examination of the various products that go to facilitate the production of counterfeit currency.

- There was distribution of misinformation and innovative use of other intelligence sources.

Counterfeit pharmaceuticals

This section of the chapter is now going to focus on investigation into the illicit trade in pharmaceuticals. It will identify what part technology and the Internet play in such offences and will show you how to investigate such crimes from a technical aspect, and what part digital intelligence and forensics play. These investigative strategies can also be used against other counterfeiting offences associated with the Internet.

Counterfeit pharmaceutical data is currently limited, fragmented and at times shrouded in secrecy. In addition, problems are sometimes defined by reference to a number of familiar instances, rather than fact. If facts are presented, they can on occasions appear as optimistic and highly questionable estimates.

Crime trends

Organised crime and criminals do not stand still and the history of crime trends shows how they have transcended different crimes in order to maximise profit and minimise any potential prison time.

- **Armed robbery**: In 1964, some of those who took part in the Great Train Robbery received 30-year prison sentences (BBC, 1964).

- **Controlled drugs**: A kilo of cocaine can be bought for around £39,000. However, those dealing in such commodities face the potential of life imprisonment (DrugScope, 2009).

- **Cigarettes, perfume and counterfeit currency**: For the production and supply of counterfeit currency, a person convicted on indictment can receive up to ten years' imprisonment (Spot Counterfeits, 2006).

- **Counterfeit pharmaceuticals**: A kilo of the active ingredient for 'Viagra' costs about £70 and can make well over 10,000 tablets, with a resale value of £10 a tablet. Those involved can heighten their chances of evading capture by living in country A, banking in countries B, C and D, buying the ingredients in multiple countries, hosting the sales website in country E, and moving the website regularly, thereby exploiting the voids created by national and jurisdictional boundaries.

> *It's estimated that 90% of counterfeit drugs are sold on the Internet, 44% of Internet Viagra is fake, the global sale of counterfeit drugs will reach $75 billion this year and EU seizures have risen dramatically.*
>
> (Alphagalileo, 2010)

The current regulatory environment makes the illicit trade in pharmaceuticals attractive to criminals for a variety of reasons:

- the globalisation of industry, which has relaxed the barriers to trade, thus facilitating the circulation of counterfeit products;

- the opportunity to operate internationally or through the Internet and, therefore, outside the jurisdiction of national regulators;

- the ability to introduce counterfeit at all stages of the supply network – manufacturer distribution and entry through wholesalers, pharmacies, the black market and the Internet;

- it is a lucrative activity, with little risk of being caught;

- it is also linked to various forms of organised crime, which operate across borders with ease.

Those who participate in this illicit trade are criminals and opportunists, who operate globally and have little regard for public health. They are becoming increasingly sophisticated, nevertheless a given element still produce their illegal products in squalid surroundings.

They then distribute the counterfeit products through multiple channels, mainly paths of least resistance, where there is limited law enforcement activity and where there are free trade zones. In addition, they have entered counterfeit pharmaceuticals into legitimate distribution channels. The participants will target any pharmaceutical product and will exploit any weaknesses. The following are examples of those weaknesses that we find mainly in the developing countries:

- poor state of the economy and low income per capita;

- pharmaceutical smuggling across borders;

- lack of pharmaceutical retail outlets;

- lack of access to many pharmaceutical products, making low-priced counterfeit ones attractive;

- lack of education about the danger of counterfeit pharmaceuticals;

- lack of awareness by consumers of the legislation relating to counterfeit pharmaceuticals;

- corruption;

- lack of collaboration between different regulatory agencies;

- weak laws, enforcement and penalties;

- lack of surveillance at points of entry.

What we do know is that the problem is a global one that affects both developed and undeveloped countries to varying degrees, but how far does the problem reach?

What is the extent of the problem?

According to the World Health Organization, those most affected include Africa, Asia and Latin America (WHO, 2010). But the true extent of the problem of counterfeit pharmaceuticals is not really known. Counterfeiting is an underworld activity and, as such, it is hard to detect and investigate. Moreover, countries and companies that detect the problem do not always report an incident. So, it is hard to know or even estimate the true extent of the problem.

What we do know is that counterfeiting is getting worse. The Center for Medicine in the Public Interest projects counterfeit sales of $75 billion in 2010, a 92 per cent increase since 2005 (CMPI, 2009).

The counterfeiting of medical products needs to be taken very seriously, as it constitutes a significant threat to patient safety and public health. The consequences of counterfeiting pharmaceuticals, in addition to endangering the well-being and lives of the general public, are:

- loss of confidence both by the medical profession and by the public in the authenticity and safety of medicines;

- infringement of intellectual property rights;

- damage to the reputation of the genuine products involved and, consequently, the investment made by the pharmaceutical industry.

Whatever the proportion of counterfeit products, there can be serious health implications for patients. This is particularly the case if the counterfeit does not contain the active ingredient or sufficient quantity of the genuine product. Even if a counterfeit product contains the same active ingredient as the genuine product, it will present a safety risk, because there will have been no control over the supply source, or manufacturing process, or other processes imposed on the manufacturer of the genuine product. Counterfeiters do not adopt these rigorous manufacturing practices.

Counterfeit pharmaceuticals can also cause organisations to be ordered to recall medicines, or specified batch numbers, from the shelves. This can be very expensive for the organisation, especially because they have to store the said pharmaceuticals until they are given the all-clear or have to be destroyed.

PRACTICAL TASK

Access the following online resources and then answer the questions below.

www.psi-inc.org/index.cfm

www.who.int/mediacentre/factsheets/fs275/en/index.html

- *What is a counterfeit pharmaceutical?*
- *How big is the problem?*
- *What is the geographical distribution of the problem?*
- *What is the difficulty in defining the extent of the problem?*

Pharmaceuticals are deliberately and fraudulently mislabelled with respect to identity and/or source. Counterfeiting can apply to both branded and generic products, and counterfeit pharmaceuticals may include products with the correct ingredients but fake packaging, with the wrong ingredients, without active ingredients, or with insufficient active ingredients.

Modus operandi

Pharmaceutical theft
Pharmaceutical theft is defined as an illegal taking of medicines. Thefts include burglary, robbery and fraud. The responsible individuals may be insiders such as employees, or outsiders such as professional thieves. The theft may occur anywhere in the distribution chain, such as at the site of manufacture, or at the freight forwarder, distribution centre, warehouse, pharmacy or hospital.

Diversion
The prices of pharmaceuticals are reduced when selling to the United Nations, WHO, a third-world country or similar. Between the sale and arrival at their intended destination, they are stolen by thieves or corrupt officials. Counterfeits can be and are introduced and delivered to the intended destination, while the originals are resold.

Distribution channels and parallel trade
Distribution channels can be either legitimate or illegitimate.

- **Legitimate**: pharmaceuticals are distributed within a government-regulated supply chain, which attempts to ensure the integrity of the product and packaging at every stage.

- **Illegitimate**: pharmaceuticals are distributed through non-regulated channels, which do not guarantee product integrity or consumer safety, and where financial motivation is a driving factor.

Parallel trade causes a problem, as it can be lawful in some countries and unlawful in others, thus creating a void that can be, and is, exploited by organised crime. Typically, a company negotiates the price of a drug with the Ministry of Health in the UK or its equivalent in other countries around the world. The prices will vary; for example, Greece is one of the cheapest, so it pays to buy in Greece and transport them elsewhere. It also creates opportunities to inject counterfeit products into the distribution system.

Genuine pharmaceuticals should go directly from the drug company to the wholesaler and then to the pharmacy or hospital. However, in reality, they will change hands six or seven times before they get to the consumer. Wherever there is a change of hands, there is an opportunity for counterfeits to be introduced.

Counterfeit labels and packaging
Counterfeiters, at times, put more resources into the counterfeiting of labels and packaging than into the product itself. Genuine drugs will also be relabelled, so as to

cover up past expiration dates or to claim higher amounts of the active ingredient. Counterfeiters generally deal not only with counterfeit products, but with diverted, expired and stolen products as well. They employ state-of-the-art computer technologies, such as desktop publishing, to produce counterfeit labels that are indistinguishable from the genuine, original labels.

Sources of intelligence

The Pharmaceutical Security Institute (PSI) is a non-profit organisation that is dedicated to protecting public health, sharing information on counterfeit pharmaceuticals and initiating enforcement actions through the appropriate authorities.

In 2002, and in conjunction with its members, the PSI developed a Counterfeiting Incident System (CIS), which is a vital online tool for the collecting of information and intelligence.

Then, in 2005, PSI inaugurated the Internet Investigative Inquiry File (I3F). The I3F is a data file containing information and intelligence that is related to the investigation of suspicious websites advertising pharmaceuticals for sale. The I3F is separate from the CIS and was established following a significant increase in member Internet-related inquiries. It has become a valuable tool in connecting investigations, and it facilitates the sharing of information related to each member's experience in conducting Internet investigations of particular Internet websites.

Other sources of intelligence, both digital and real time, can involve the following types of criminal:

- those who are arrested or known to be in possession of counterfeit pharmaceuticals (the price paid per item compared to its street value will indicate where the individual stands in relation to the supply chain);

- those who distribute counterfeit pharmaceuticals (the price paid, and the number of items held, will indicate how close the individual is to the source of the counterfeit pharmaceuticals);

- those who are responsible for the production of counterfeit pharmaceuticals;

- those who are arrested or known to be involved in financing the production and/or distribution of counterfeit pharmaceuticals;

- those who are suspected of, or known to be gaining from, the production and distribution of counterfeit pharmaceuticals;

- those who help facilitate the production and distribution of counterfeit pharmaceuticals.

Additional intelligence sources

Most counterfeiters want to get the amount of active ingredient correct, as this makes for repeat business, but there are other potential sources of intelligence, such as the categorisation of packaging and content; as with counterfeit currency, indicatives could be created. Other areas include the use of sales analysis; that is, when complaints are received that the sales of normally high-volume pharmaceuticals are slowing down considerably and for no apparent reason, scanning and tracking takes place of products, customers and the public as a whole, traders and stakeholders, genuine e-pharmacies and e-doctors, informants and tasked witnesses.

The Internet

The Internet is a key enabler in connecting counterfeiters and illicit traders with one another and with unwitting patients and customers. On the Internet, you can obtain almost any pharmaceutical you want – legally or illegally.

Consumers purchasing pharmaceuticals directly from Internet websites have no idea of how or where the counterfeit drugs they are buying are manufactured. It is not a new phenomenon. The most common Internet counterfeits are drugs related to 'lifestyle' problems, such as impotence, obesity and baldness. Apart from Viagra, other favourites are weight-loss drugs such as Ephedra, and male hair-loss treatments such as Propecia. Internet prescribing can be extremely safe if you are ethical and have guidelines. Unfortunately, the growth of Internet pharmacies has created an opportunity for those who trade in illicit pharmaceuticals.

Terrorists

A terrorist organisation, with limited technical skills, could set up an online pharmacy, generate a customer base, and then deliver tainted goods to unwitting consumers from virtually anywhere in the world.

Children and teenagers

Teenagers and even young children in search of a fix now have unprecedented access to addictive drugs, mind-stimulating prescription uppers and body-bulking anabolic steroids. Some sites and message boards actually coach teens in the process of ordering steroids, uppers and sex-enhancement contraband. These websites have also been known to offer their customers encrypted email.

Problems in controlling Internet trade in pharmaceuticals

Counterfeiting, illegal diversion and distribution on the Internet have become major global problems for all involved, and are further complicated by:

- servers located in other countries;
- websites opening and closing easily;
- lack of cooperation and collaboration among relevant agencies;
- limited resources to combat the problem;
- lack of international cooperation;
- difficulty in apprehending offenders;
- ease of setting up and providing a convincing shop window;
- jurisdictional problems for law enforcement.

Customers and e-doctors

Customers are lured by relentless spam, low prices and breakdowns in doctor–patient relationships, and e-doctors capitalise on this.

- On average they evaluate 300 applications a day.
- They are paid between £5 and £80 per application.
- One physician can rubber-stamp over 1,000 applications a day.
- Patients have no way to screen a prescribing e-doctor's credentials.
- Doctors who want to get into the Internet trade respond to ads posted on websites.
- Sometimes doctors solicit e-pharmacies directly to become prescribing doctors.

E-pharmacies

An e-pharmacy sells medications through its website. Some of these pharmacies are simply the cyberspace version of traditional bricks and mortar pharmacies. Others exist only in the cyberworld and prescriptions are filled and shipped from a warehouse. The latter type of Internet pharmacy lacks fixed costs such as property leases, maintenance charges and property taxes. On average, it takes only ten minutes to place an order. Some have created groups, such as the Center for Information Therapy (www.ixcenter.org/), in order to set guidelines in an attempt to police their own industry.

Telepharmacies

A telepharmacy is a pharmaceutical care system in which pharmacists in a central location use ICT to oversee pharmacy business and provide patient services, including prescription dispensing. It has evolved and come into prominence because the supply of pharmacists cannot meet demand. It also provides a new and unique opportunity for criminal abuse.

Other preventative measures

The National Association of Boards of Pharmacy (NABP) is an internationally independent association that assists others in developing and implementing standards for the purpose of protecting the health of people around the world.

In response to public concern over the safety of online pharmacies, the NABP created the Verified Internet Pharmacy Practice Sites (VIPPS) programme, and pharmacies that display the VIPPS seal have demonstrated to the NABP their compliance with VIPPS criteria.

There are currently two categories that Internet pharmacies fall into: those that the NABP recommend for the public to use, because they are accredited through the VIPPS programme; and those that have not achieved such accreditation.

In December 2009, the NABP review of websites that sell prescription pharmaceuticals listed more than 5,000 Internet outlets as 'not recommended'. In addition, 96 per cent of the total number of websites reviewed were found not to comply with pharmacy laws and standards that were established in the USA to safeguard public health (NABP, 2009).

The Medical Health Regulatory Authority (MHRA) mission in the UK is to safeguard the health of the public by ensuring that medicines and medical devices work, and that they are acceptably safe. As part of that role, it repeatedly monitors Internet websites, particularly those known to be selling prescription-only medicines, and frequent checks are made to see if these websites are based in the UK. Those that are located overseas have their details given to the appropriate regulatory body in that country.

The MHRA has carried out a number of actions that have resulted in coordinated activity against those websites most active in the UK that are suspected of breaches of medicine regulation. During this enforcement work, observers from other enforcement teams and the media have accompanied the MHRA. This is in an effort to raise awareness of the increased risk in purchasing pharmaceuticals from unlicensed websites operated by unqualified individuals (MHRA, 2009).

WHO has confronted this predicament by creating an international partnership of stakeholders called the International Medical Products Anti-Counterfeiting Taskforce (IMPACT). The taskforce was created in 2006 and has been energetic in forging worldwide teamwork to seek global solutions to this global challenge and in raising understanding of the dangers of counterfeit pharmaceutical products. The partnership consists of all the major anti-counterfeiting players, including international organisations, non-governmental organisations, enforcement agencies, and pharmaceutical manufacturers, associations and regulatory authorities (IMPACT, 2010).

To help prevent the distribution of counterfeit products, pharmaceutical organisations will use recordation to combat their importation. This enables owners to record their trademarks and copyrights, therefore making it easier to identify fakes at borders. Industry will have in-house lawyers or a worldwide company that will be the single point of contact for customs purposes.

All measures that cut the profit margins for manufacturing fakes, such as reducing the price and increasing the availability of genuine, quality-assured drugs, will make counterfeiting a less attractive criminal activity. However, there might be a 'Gresham's Law' at work; that is, bad pharmaceuticals drive good pharmaceuticals out of local circulation. Good drugs may be withheld and diverted to more profitable markets. This law is commonly stated as: 'When there is a legal tender currency, bad money drives good money out of circulation' (Britannica, 2010).

Unfortunately, regulatory tools do not reach beyond country borders. Combating the unlawful activities of foreign-based Internet pharmacies requires worldwide cooperation among individual countries as each mandates and enforces its own set of medicine and pharmacy regulations.

Thus, the answer lies with lead countries, pharmaceutical organisations and pharmaceutical companies, which need to establish and enforce regulatory plans that can serve as models to other countries. These efforts, combined with a consumer education campaign emphasising the potential dangers of ordering pharmaceuticals online, will help curb their damaging effects.

The US Congress passed the Ryan Haight Online Pharmacy Consumer Protection Act in 2008. It amends the Controlled Substances Act to prohibit the delivery, distribution or dispensing of a controlled substance that is a prescription drug over the Internet without a valid prescription.

Access the Internet using Google or a similar search engine and find out why the legislation is called 'Ryan Haight', which pharmaceutical was involved and what caused this legislation to be created.

- The Dutch Healthcare Inspectorate gave a warning in 2006 not to buy 'Tamiflu' through the Internet. This was as a result of counterfeit capsules in the Netherlands being found to contain lactose and vitamin C, but no active ingredient (WHO, 2006). In the same year, UK officials seized 5,000 packets of counterfeit 'Tamiflu', which were estimated to be worth £500,000 (Swinford and Leake, 2006).

- In 2006, a US federal investigation led to the arrest of Richard Cowley in the state of Washington. His source of supply and others were arrested in China, where officials seized 444,000 counterfeit 'Cialis' pills, hundreds of pill bottles, information inserts and hologram seals. The undercover operation against him saw contact by way of his website and email address. Records obtained during the course of the investigation disclosed that Cowley used the same Internet website to contact his suppliers in China in order to place orders received via his website. The labels, packaging and seals were also determined to be counterfeit (People's Daily Online, 2005).

- In 2010, the US Food and Drug Administration (FDA) issued a press release that reported a number of cases in which individuals who had purchased pharmaceuticals online or over the phone, through so-called 'telepharmacies', were later called by a person claiming to be an FDA agent. This alleged agent intimidates people with scare tactics about the illegality of their purchase, and threatens legal action unless a fine is paid. The fine will range from $100 to $250,000, the FDA said, and in some cases individuals have had charges made to their credit cards to cover the so-called fines. Others are told to wire the payments to the Dominican Republic. If victims decline to send the money, they are often threatened with a search of their property, arrest or physical harm (The Tech Herald, 2010).

PRACTICAL TASK

Go to www.who.int/impact/news/WebINTERPOLmediarelease.pdf and read through these 2008 global investigations into counterfeit pharmaceuticals, in particular the article entitled 'Illegal online medicine suppliers targeted in first international Internet day of action'. The operation focused on those individuals behind Internet websites that sold and supplied unlicensed or prescription-only medicines claiming to treat a range of ailments. From the content you will see the success an internationally coordinated day of action can have.

CHAPTER SUMMARY

A successful implementation of a cyber-crime strategy will assist governments and international organisations to determine the precise extent and nature of the various counterfeiting problems. It will also go towards reinforcing the fact that there is a need for interested parties to exchange information and intelligence.

There is clearly a need to scope the illicit trade in counterfeit, because the true size of the problem is not evident from all the data gathered to date. What can be said is that there have been documented increases in the number of incidents worldwide, there are more countries experiencing counterfeiting than ever before, and there is an even wider variety of products being counterfeited, illegally diverted and stolen.

In those countries with active enforcement programmes, the investigators need to intensify their efforts at coordination and reach beyond the retailers and distributors in order to identify the manufacturers of counterfeit products. This is the most effective way to dismantle these organised criminal groups, which operate on a multinational basis.

This chapter has given you an understanding of the methods of operation of organised counterfeiting groups, and has emphasised the point that increased international coordination and collaboration by law enforcement agencies and public/private partnerships will be the only way to address these types of crime.

In addition, you can now see that new technologies need and should be introduced to ensure that counterfeiting and IP crimes do not get out of control and seriously undermine economies or public health and safety. You have also seen how offenders are able to elude arrest and prosecution by shifting their operations from location to location and by taking advantage of delays in the investigation process.

The tasks completed will have provided you with an insight into how technology and the Internet assist the commission of a wide range of counterfeiting offences. The content of the chapter has been limited to a number of those offences; however, they are the most serious and the ones that have the most impact on society.

REFERENCES

Alphagalileo (2010) Counterfeit internet drugs pose significant risks and discourage vital health checks. Available online at www.alphagalileo.org/ViewItem.aspx?ItemId=66446&CultureCode=en (accessed 22 January 2010).

Bank of England (2009) Counterfeit Bank of England banknotes. Available online at www.bankofengland.co.uk/banknotes/about/counterfeits.htm (accessed 22 January 2010).

BBC (1964) 1964: 'Great Train Robbers' get 300 years, *On This Day*, April 16. Available online at http://news.bbc.co.uk/onthisday/hi/dates/stories/april/16/newsid_2488000/2488041.stm (accessed 22 January 2010).

Britannica (2010) Gresham's Law. Available online at www.britannica.com/EBchecked/topic/245850/Greshams-law (accessed 22 January 2010).

Center for Medicine in the Public Interest (CMPI) (2009) Counterfeit drugs and China. Available online at www.cmpi.org/in-the-news/testimony/counterfeit-drugs-and-china-new/ (accessed 22 January 2010).

DrugScope (2009*)* DrugScope Street Drug Trends Survey 2009: falling illegal drug purity 'accelerates trend' in users combining different drugs. Available online at www.drugscope.org.uk/ourwork/pressoffice/pressreleases/Street_drug_trends_2009.htm (accessed 22 January 2010).

Federation Against Copyright Theft (FACT) (2010) Who we are. Available online at www.fact-uk.org.uk/index.htm (accessed 22 January 2010).

International Medical Products Anti-Counterfeiting Taskforce (IMPACT) (2010) Home page. Available online at www.who.int/impact/en/ (accessed 22 January 2010).

Interpol (2010) Intellectual property (IP) crime. Available online at www.interpol.int/Public/FinancialCrime/IntellectualProperty/Default.asp (accessed 22 January 2010).

Medical Health Regulatory Authority (MHRA) (2009) About us. Available online at www.mhra.gov.uk/Aboutus/index.htm (accessed 22 January 2010).

National Association of Boards of Pharmacy (NABP) (2009) 5,000 websites selling prescription drugs outside of pharmacy laws and practice standards. Available online at www.nabp.net/ (accessed 22 January 2010).

People's Daily Online (2005) China, US jointly seize 440,000 pills of counterfeit. Available online at http://english.peopledaily.com.cn/200509/09/eng20050909_207454.html (accessed 22 January 2010).

Spot Counterfeits (2006) *Stephen Jory: Britain's Greatest Counterfeiter?* Available online at www.spotcounterfeits.co.uk/stephen-jory-britains-greatest-counterfeiter.html (accessed 22 January 2010).

Swinford, Steven and Leake, Jonathan (2006) Black-market bird flu drug seized in raids. *The Times*, 15 January. Available online at www.timesonline.co.uk/tol/news/uk/article788697.ece (accessed 22 January 2010).

The Tech Herald (2010) FDA issues warning over online pharmacy extortion scam. Available online at www.thetechherald.com/article.php/201001/5026/FDA-issues-warning-over-online-pharmacy-extortion-scam#ixzz0dZpbWsX1 (accessed 22 January 2010).

Willis, Tom (2006) Stephen Jory: 'Lavender Hill Mob' counterfeiter. The Independent, 2 May 2006. Available online at www.independent.co.uk/news/obituaries/stephen-jory-479898.html (accessed 22 January 2010).

World Health Organization (WHO) (2006) Counterfeit medicines, fact sheet. Available online at www.who.int/medicines/services/counterfeit/impact/ImpactF_S/en/index.html (accessed 22 January 2010).

World Health Organization (WHO) (2010) Medicines: counterfeit medicines, fact sheet. Available online at www.who.int/mediacentre/factsheets/fs275/en/index.html (accessed 22 January 2010).

USEFUL WEBSITES

www.interpol.int/ (Interpol)

www.psi-inc.org/index.cfm (Pharmaceutical Security Institute)

www.who.int/impact/en/ (WHO's IMPACT website)

CASES

Regina v. *GRIMES Anthony and JONES Paul*, Southwark Crown Court (April 2001)

Regina v. *JORY Stephen, MAINSTONE Kenneth and others*, Winchester Crown Court (December 1999)

LEGISLATION

UK

Common Law (Conspiracy to defraud)

Copyright Designs & Patent Act 1988

Criminal Law Act 1977

Forgery and Counterfeiting Act 1981

Misuse of Drugs Act 1971 (s5(3): Possession with intent to supply)

Proceeds of Crime Act 2002

Theft Act 1968 (s8: Robbery)

Trade Marks Act 1994

Video Recordings Act 1984

USA

Controlled Substances Act 1970

Ryan Haight Online Pharmacy Consumer Protection Act 2008

8 Road traffic and technology

CHAPTER OBJECTIVES

By the end of this chapter you should be able to:

- understand the development and application of technological solutions for roads policing;
- describe roads policing strategy and supporting legislation;
- analyse a number of key issues relating to the use of roads policing technology and its contribution to community safety, crime reduction and investigation.

LINKS TO STANDARDS

This chapter provides opportunities for links with the following Skills for Justice, National Occupational Standards (NOS) for Policing and Law Enforcement 2008.

AE1.1   Maintain and develop your own knowledge, skills and competence.
CE101.1 Provide an initial response to road-related incidents.
CE102.1 Initiate investigations into road-related incidents.
CE304.2 Deal with the vehicle, its driver and occupants.
CE305.1 Manage road checks.
HA1   Manage your own resources.
HA2   Manage your own resources and professional development.

Introduction

Policing in the twenty-first century faces the challenge of managing problems associated with increasing ownership and use of motor vehicles within the UK, and the growth in technological solutions has provided a new landscape for policing in tackling public safety, environmental and crime issues on the roads. The array of such solutions currently available is developing at a rapid rate, with cost and training implications for the police service, and with an impact on the public who are exposed to the new technologies. For example, fixed and mobile cameras are widespread throughout the road network and add to the growing concern that we are living in a 'surveillance society' (see Chapter 6). The use of speed enforcement cameras has created much national debate and is considered by some to constitute a stealth tax on the motorist.

The motor vehicle has become an essential part of everyday life within the UK, with ownership continuing to rise to record levels. Road safety is a major issue for the police service, and the reduction of road death and injury remains a priority, even though there has been an overall drop in road death statistics. In 1926, for example, there were 1,715,000 registered vehicles in the UK, culminating in 4,886 road deaths (2.9 deaths per 1,000 vehicles). In 1997, there were 26,974,000 registered vehicles and 3,599 road deaths – the equivalent of 0.1 deaths per 1,000 vehicles (Hicks and Allen, 1999).

Recent statistics relating to vehicle registrations and driving licence holders provide evidence of continued growth (see Table 8.1).

Despite the increase in motor vehicles on UK roads, the police service has seen the demise of the traditional traffic officer. In more recent times, most police forces had dedicated traffic divisions made up of specialist officers, who were highly trained and were specifically deployed to deal with traffic-related issues, such as accident investigation, vehicle examination, traffic law enforcement, education, prevention and advice.

As government priorities and social conditions have changed, the operational demands on police officers have increased considerably. There was evidence that the numbers of specialist traffic officers were starting to decline, with police forces disbanding traffic divisions and finding new solutions for roads policing, such as technology, the use of support staff, and multi-tasking of operational police officers. Her Majesty's Inspectorate of Constabulary (HMIC) reported that most police forces had 15–20 per cent of their strength dedicated to roads policing in 1966, but by 1998 this had declined to just 7 per cent (HMIC, 1998). By 2004, it had declined by another 21 per cent (House of Commons Transport Committee, 2005).

In 2006, the House of Commons Transport Committee decided to investigate what role roads policing played in casualty reduction and how performance could be improved. Although it was recognised that road casualties had decreased, the levels were still considered to be too high (2006, p3). Table 8.2 shows how road deaths have decreased since 1971.

The Transport Committee report recognised the importance of both technology and roads police officers and that a balance was required between the two. Automatic number plate recognition (ANPR) and speed cameras were acknowledged as having made a significant

Table 8.1 Vehicle registrations and licence holders

Year	Number of licensed motor vehicles	Number of full and provisional licence holders
1990	24,673,000	33,376,606
2005	32,897,384	41,077,900
2008	34,390,302	43,450,575 (16 March 2009)

Source: DVLA, 2009.

Table 8.2 Road deaths from 1971 to 2008

Year	Number of road deaths
1971	8,302
1981	5,133
1991	5,276
1998	3,501
2008	2,538

Source: ONS (2009); DfT (2009a).

contribution to road safety, but technology had its limitations and police officers still had a key role to play.

> *The special role of roads police officers must be recognised and protected, and the high standards of roads policing – which have helped the UK's roads to be among the safest in the world – must be maintained.*

(2006, p64)

Having received evidence from a number of key organisations, the Committee provided a range of recommendations. The specialist role of roads police officers was to be maintained and protected, with no reduction in specialist training. The report also highlighted the fact that government had failed to give roads policing priority within the national policing plan and that, in future, it should be recognised as a key priority, in order to ensure that the police service continued to invest in both roads police officers and technology to meet government road safety targets. The Committee also made a series of recommendations relating to the development and use of technology that would contribute to an effective roads policing strategy.

REFLECTIVE TASK

Access the Roads Policing and Technology *report at www.publications.parliament.uk/pa/cm200506/cmselect/cmtran/975/975.pdf and read through the section, 'Conclusions and recommendations' on pages 64–73.*

- *Make a list of the references to technology and consider how they will contribute to achieving the right balance between the deployment of roads police officers and technology.*

- *Consider the options suggested for development and use of technology and how this may impact on both the motorist and the future role of policing.*

You will have found that the potential of technology is likely to have a considerable impact on the motorist, with the development of devices such as drug-screening equipment, intelligent speed adaption and alcolocks.

ACPO, the Department for Transport (DfT) and the Home Office published a roads policing strategy in 2007 with five priorities:

- denying criminals the use of the road by enforcing the law;

- reducing road casualties;

- tackling the threat of terrorism;

- reducing the antisocial use of vehicles;

- enhancing public confidence and reassurance by patrolling the roads.

(adapted from ACPO, 2007, p12)

The development of technology will contribute to achieving some of these priorities and the following specific areas of police investigation and road traffic law enforcement will be explored during the remainder of the chapter, in order to highlight how the technology is attempting to contribute to an effective and efficient way of making the roads within the UK safer. We will discuss:

- road safety cameras;

- automatic number plate recognition (ANPR);

- road traffic collision investigation;

- driving under the influence of drink or drugs.

Road safety cameras

The use of road safety cameras has become one of the most controversial areas of policing during the past decade. Such cameras can be used to detect both speeding offences and the crossing of red traffic lights. The cameras can be fixed, mobile or designed to record average speed (time over distance).

REFLECTIVE TASK

- *Consider the use of road safety cameras. Do they contribute to making the roads safer or do they persecute the motorist and provide a welcome cash flow for government? Make a list of the advantages and disadvantages of this kind of approach and make an argument for or against the technology.*

- *Now compare your argument with the DfT, which provides clear evidence of the benefits of the approach. You can access the relevant section of the DfT website at www.dft.gov.uk/pgr/roadsafety/speedmanagement/safetycamerasfrequentlyasked4603.*

Legislation

The use of road safety cameras and associated offences are governed by a number of Acts of Parliament and the following is a summary of some of the key legislation.

- **Road Traffic Regulation Act 1984**: sections 81–89 and schedule 6 provide for speed limits on restricted roads, powers for local authorities to vary speed limits, setting of speed limits for certain types of motor vehicles, exemptions from speed limits and the offence of exceeding a speed limit.

- **Road Traffic Offenders Act 1988**: section 20 provides that a device designed or adapted for measuring the speed of a motor vehicle by radar must be approved by the Secretary of State.

- **Road Traffic Act 1988**: section 36 provides for the offence of failing to comply with a traffic sign that includes traffic lights.

- **Road Traffic Act 1991**: section 23 allows evidence produced by a prescribed device (e.g., speed or traffic light camera) to be admissible in court. The device must be approved by the Secretary of State and any conditions subject to the approval must be satisfied.

- **Vehicles (Crime) Act 2001**: section 38 allows the Secretary of State to provide funds to public authorities for the prevention, detection and enforcement of speeding and traffic lights offences.

Safety camera partnerships

Following the legislation in 1991 that allowed evidence to be produced in court from type-approved safety cameras (a safety camera describes both a speed and traffic light camera), the first cameras were installed in West London in 1992. Twenty-one speed cameras were introduced, together with 12 traffic light cameras (Ward, 2003, p1). Their effectiveness was monitored and, following positive results, the use of safety cameras spread throughout the UK.

The early schemes were managed by the local authority, which had the responsibility for purchasing and installing the safety camera equipment. The police were responsible for installing and changing the film, and for processing offenders. All money raised from fines at this time was taken by the Treasury.

PRACTICAL TASK

Access the Police Research Series Paper 20 of 1996, which can be found at www.home office.gov.uk/rds/prgpdfs/fprs20.pdf. Read through the executive summary and identify what the authors say are the benefits of safety cameras.

You will have noted that evidence was provided that, where the cameras were situated, they reduced road accidents and average speed. You will also have seen a breakdown of the costs involved and how these were split between the local authority and the police. Cost was clearly an issue and, despite the evidence that the cameras were making a significant contribution to road safety, further deployment of cameras throughout the UK was being hampered by the cost and resource implications. As a result of this, the government provided a 'Netting off' scheme, which allowed some of the fixed penalty revenue to be retained to cover installation, management and processing costs, with the aim of encouraging more use.

In April 2000, a pilot of eight safety camera partnerships was introduced, made up of representatives from the local authority, the police, the magistrate's court, and other agencies such as the health authority. Following evidence of the effectiveness of this type of partnership approach, a national safety camera programme created 38 schemes between 2001 and 2004 in England and Wales. Table 8.3 provides evidence of the increase in numbers of road safety cameras between 2000 and 2006.

Alistair Darling (the then Secretary of State for Transport) announced a further change in funding in December 2005 and also provided evidence of the effectiveness of the 38 safety camera partnerships, following research that stated that the cameras continued to be highly effective in reducing speeding, accidents and casualties. The following figures were published:

- the number of vehicles exceeding the speed limit fell by 70 per cent at fixed camera sites;

- there was a 22 per cent reduction in personal injury collisions, equating to 4,230 per year;

- there was a 42 per cent reduction in people killed or seriously injured, equating to 1,745 per year including over 100 deaths.

(adapted from DfT, 2009c)

The national safety camera programme has now been replaced by partnerships that take a more holistic view of road safety issues and develop a range of strategies to reduce road casualties, which still includes the use of road safety cameras. The government now provides funds to local authorities based on their road safety needs.

Table 8.3 Numbers of road safety cameras from 2000 to 2006

Type of camera	2000	2006
Fixed	1,295	2,544
Mobile	173	2,373
Red light	464	600
Other types	3	45
Totals:	1,935	5,562

Source: DfT (2009b).

PRACTICAL TASK

Go to http://microsites.lincolnshire.gov.uk/LRSP, which is the Lincolnshire Police road safety partnership website. This will provide you with an example of an integrated approach for tackling road safety issues

Identify the organisations involved, the different people or specialists used, the methods adopted, and how technology assists the overall strategy.

Other speed devices

Technology continues to develop at a rapid pace and, in addition to fixed, mobile and time over distance speed cameras, there is a range of other technology that can be used for detecting speeding offences.

There are currently nearly 50 different speeding devices that have been type-approved by the Home Office. When a device is produced it is first considered by the ACPO Road Policing Enforcement Technology Committee, which will consider the technical description, look at health and safety issues, and test its operational viability. If the device is recommended, it is then considered by the Home Office Scientific Development Branch, which may carry out further tests on the device. If it is satisfied, the device will be recommended for type approval.

PRACTICAL TASK

Go to http://police.homeoffice.gov.uk/publications/road-traffic-documents/approved-speed-meters/) and identify the range of speeding devices that are approved by the Home Office.

In addition to the safety cameras, some police officers have access to in-car and hand-held devices for speed detection. Hand-held devices are now available to local volunteers as part of a scheme called Community Speed Watch, whereby they can contribute to improving road safety.

The use of a helicopter is another innovative way of detecting and deterring speeding offences and, in August 2008, Essex Police announced that they were carrying out aerial speed checks to improve road safety by fitting radar and number plate recognition technology to their helicopter (www.thisistotalessex.co.uk, 2008).

Prevention can make a significant impact in any strategy being developed to improve road safety. Many companies are now fitting speed restriction devices (speed limiters) to their vehicles to save fuel costs and to discourage employees from speeding.

The use of intelligent road studs provides further opportunities for warning drivers of dangers and the studs can also be used for speed enforcement. They can contain lighting systems, weather and road condition sensors, infra-red speed detectors and digital video cameras that can be routed through to roadside cabinets and traffic control systems.

The development of global positioning system (GPS) technology is now providing some excellent opportunities to prevent drivers from speeding. The technology (known as intelligent speed adaptation) links the vehicle to the GPS satellite through a road mapping digital system that has knowledge of speed limits. The system can be linked to the vehicle controls to prevent the speed limit from being exceeded. Initial research completed by the University of Leeds, in conjunction with the Motor Industry Research Association (MIRA), has suggested that road injuries could reduce by 36 per cent and fatalities by 59 per cent if the scheme was made mandatory (Carston and Fowkes, 2000, p22).

REFLECTIVE TASK

The use of mandatory intelligent speed adaptation may be considered by some to be a further erosion of our civil liberties and a step too far in the challenge of reducing road casualties.

Consider the impact of this type of technology and make a list of what you consider to be the advantages and disadvantages of the approach. Compare your answers with comments made in the two articles and video clip that can be found at:

- *www.guardian.co.uk/commentisfree/2008/dec/30/motoring-transport*

- *http://news.bbc.co.uk/1/hi/uk/7803997.stm.*

The introduction and use of this type of technology could provide a useful basis for an academic debate within an assignment.

Automatic number plate recognition

ANPR was first developed in 1976 by the Police Scientific Development Branch and the first prototypes were being tested in 1979 with early trials on the A1 and in the Dartford tunnel. The technology provides a mass surveillance method using optical character recognition to read vehicle registration marks. The technology can scan over 3,000 vehicles per minute at speeds of up to 100 mph and then check the registration marks against a number of databases that contain information such as stolen cars, disqualified drivers, vehicles without tax, insurance and test certificates, and arrest warrants. ANPR is used widely by the police service and a number of other organisations for a variety of purposes, such as the prevention and detection of crime, tackling vehicle congestion and emissions, and managing parking.

The initial use of ANPR during the 1980s was in support of counter-terrorism initiatives. The technology was used covertly and was very expensive. Today's ANPR technology is smaller, faster, more reliable and relatively inexpensive. The police service quickly recognised the potential of the technology not only for tackling terrorism, but also for the prevention and detection of crime and the reduction of road casualties. By 1999, 15 police forces were using ANPR with eight further forces considering its use (ACPO, 2004, p2).

The government quickly realised that ANPR could make a significant contribution to preventing crime and increasing detection rates. Project Spectrum was introduced in June 2002 and £4.65 million was made available to police forces from the crime reduction programme, with each force in England and Wales being equipped with a fully compatible mobile ANPR unit and associated back-office facility (the back-office facility is software that provides the capability of storage, matching and reporting of ANPR data).

This was quickly followed in September of the same year by Project Laser, with the government providing further funding to support nine forces taking part in a pilot scheme over six months to establish best practice use of ANPR technology. Former Home Office minister, John Denham, said:

> *Automatic Number Plate Recognition is an invaluable tool in the campaign to make our streets safer. These pilots mark the beginning of an ambitious programme of crime reduction measures, harnessing the powers of technology to drive down crime. By denying criminals use of the road the police will be better able to enforce the law, prevent crime and detect offenders.*

(cited in Community Justice Portal, 2002)

Project Laser was a resounding success and produced some outstanding results, including in excess of 100 arrests per officer per year – ten times the national average. In addition, 39,000 vehicles were stopped, resulting in 3,071 arrests, 328 stolen vehicles were recovered, and there were 101 recoveries of stolen goods and 211 drug seizures (Home Office, 2003).

In June 2003, a second phase of Project Laser was launched, including a further 14 police forces (23 in total), with funding being supplemented by ANPR fixed penalty revenue aligned to the 'Netting off' scheme (see page 124).

More success followed and the results from the evaluation of the project evidenced how powerful ANPR could be for the future of policing. Clear links between motoring offences and crime were established, mirroring previous research (see www.homeoffice.gov.uk/rds/pdfs/hors206.pdf), and the evaluation report (PA Consulting Group, 2005) highlighted a number of clear benefits for the police service:

- improving accuracy of criminal intelligence data;
- providing reassurance policing;
- dealing with unsafe vehicles and drivers;
- providing evidence to link vehicles to locations.

PRACTICAL TASK

Go to www.acpo.police.uk/asp/policies/Data/ANPR_genesis.pdf and download ACPO's Practice Advice on the Management and Use of ANPR. Go to appendix 1 (page 51) and read through the case studies, which will give you a range of ways in which ANPR can be used for investigative, intelligence and community safety purposes.

It is clear that the use of ANPR can significantly contribute to both tackling the problem of crime and enhancing road safety. Not surprisingly, when ACPO published their ANPR strategy in 2005, the link between the roads and crime became the central feature, with their strategic aim of 'Denying criminals the use of the road' (ACPO, 2005, p2).

In 2004, the Home Office provided a further £15 million to expand the ANPR scheme to other police forces, and also to create a national ANPR data centre that now sits at Hendon alongside the Police National Computer. The database stores millions of vehicle registration numbers recorded on a daily basis from a network of cameras situated throughout the UK. The stored data can be useful for both intelligence and evidence, for post-incident investigation, and to support work in tackling terrorism and organised crime. The database is not without controversy and, similarly to the CCTV debate about the surveillance society (see Chapter 6) and the national DNA database, public concerns relating to issues such as privacy, security and accuracy of data have been raised by media and civil liberty organisations.

REFLECTIVE TASK

Make a list of the advantages and the disadvantages of increasing the use of ANPR technology on UK roads, and the storing and recording of millions of vehicle registration numbers within a national database. Compare your answers with concerns raised by the media, civil liberty groups and public blogs (a search via Google or Bing using 'National ANPR Data Centre' will provide a number of useful links to relevant articles).

Also visit the BBC website at news.bbc.co.uk/1/hi/programmes/whos_watching_you/ 8064333.stm for further information and a video clip. Hear what the Information Commissioner and the Home Secretary had to say in May 2009 about some of the concerns relating to ANPR use.

A further evaluation of the use of ANPR was completed in 2007, providing more evidence of its capabilities and claiming that ANPR had delivered its highest performance outcomes since the beginning of Project Laser:

- 20,592 arrests including 5 per cent prolific or priority offenders;
- 52,037 vehicle-related document offences;
- 41,268 vehicles seized for document offences;
- 2,021 stolen vehicles recovered.

(adapted from PA Consulting, 2007, p7)

Currently, ANPR data is obtained from dedicated cameras found at fixed sites or installed within vehicles. It is also being incorporated into many existing video feeds attached to established CCTV cameras. The police service regularly carries out intercept operations, using teams of police officers to stop vehicles of interest identified by the ANPR technology. Most police forces have a number of police patrol vehicles fitted with ANPR technology, providing immediate information to the driver that can be effectively used for targeted intelligence-led patrols.

It is now common to see the police working in conjunction with other organisations, such as the Vehicle and Operator Services Agency (VOSA), the Driver and Vehicle Licensing Agency (DVLA) or HM Revenue and Customs, with ANPR technology to assist with vehicle checks and other operations relating to road safety.

In addition to the police, other organisations use ANPR technology for a variety of purposes. The following four examples show how it is used to assist with security, traffic congestion, vehicle emissions and car parking.

Central London congestion charging scheme

The central London congestion charging scheme was introduced in February 2003 with the aim of reducing traffic by 10–15 per cent and the time spent in traffic delays by 20–30 per cent. It covers an area of eight square miles and ANPR cameras are placed at all entry and exit points on the perimeter of the congestion zone. The size of the zone was doubled in February 2007 with the western extension.

Drivers are required to pay the charge in advance and, as they enter the congestion zone, the vehicle registration mark is read by a camera and checked against a database containing details of all of the vehicles that have paid or which are exempt from the charge. If the charge has not been paid, a fine is sent to the registered keeper of the vehicle.

PRACTICAL TASK

Transport for London (TfL) provides a leaflet to explain the congestion charging scheme. Download the leaflet at www.tfl.gov.uk/assets/downloads/CC-Cameras.pdf and find out how TfL deals with the issue of privacy regarding images and requests for data by third parties.

Trafford Centre, Manchester

The Trafford Centre attracts up to 20 million shoppers per year and provides 12,000 car parking spaces. Vehicle crime was a particular problem and, in 2003, ANPR technology was integrated with an already established CCTV system. In November 2007, it was reported that vehicle crime had been cut by 65 per cent, with over 100 stolen vehicles recovered and over 100 offenders arrested since the introduction of ANPR (www.public technology.net, 2007).

London's low emission zone

It has long been recognised that London suffers poor air quality and, in September 2002, the then Mayor of London, Ken Livingstone, introduced the council's air quality strategy, which claimed that the primary cause of poor air quality in London was emissions from road traffic (Livingstone, 2002, p1).

The strategy identified a range of actions to reduce emissions that included the congestion scheme and a low emission zone. The zone was introduced to the Greater London area in February 2008, targeting lorries over 12 tons and, in July 2008, lorries over 3½ tons together with buses and coaches. Vehicles not meeting the emissions criteria pay a fee for entry into the zone, which is policed by a network of ANPR cameras that link directly to a database containing information provided by VOSA, DVLA, the Society of Motor Manufacturers and Traders (SMMT) and vehicle operators.

Car parking and traffic management

ANPR provides many opportunities for the effective control and management of car parking. It also has a range of uses for contributing to effective traffic management. Some examples of its use are set out below.

- **Pre-booking technology**: paying for car parking space on the Internet. When a vehicle approaches a car park, a camera recognises the vehicle registration number (VRN) and opens the barrier.

- **Security**: providing an audit trail of all vehicles entering and leaving a car park and creating deterrence for criminals and investigation opportunities for law enforcement.

- **Fine collection**: a camera records the VRN when a car enters a car park and again upon leaving. If the time allowed for parking is exceeded, the VRN details are retained for processing a fine.

- **Toll roads**: for charging and allowing fast lane use for prepayments.

- **Journey time measurement**: assessing journey times and providing information to the motorist, such as electronic boards on motorways informing drivers how long it will take to reach a certain junction.

- **Bus lane control**: detecting vehicles breaching the lane restriction and providing details of VRNs for processing of fines.

Road traffic collision investigation

One of the core roles of an operational police officer is to deal with the many road collisions that occur on a daily basis throughout the UK. Section 170 of the Road Traffic Act 1988 requires the driver of a motor vehicle involved in a road collision to stop, provide certain information and, in certain circumstances, report the collision to the police.

The investigation of a road collision can be time-consuming and in certain cases complex. This section provides information about some of the technology that is available or is being developed to assist police officers with their investigative duties. It will specifically examine technology being developed for traffic collision recording and technology that is used for investigation at the collision scene.

Road traffic collision recording

Recording of road traffic collisions is required for a number of reasons, such as investigating the causes of a collision, preparing reports for a court or the coroner, analysis of statistics for road safety purposes, performance targets, and to inform development of road safety strategies.

Road collision recording requires the completion of many forms, and difficulties have been highlighted with timeliness, accuracy and collation of the information submitted. Sir Ronnie Flanagan, in his review of policing published in 2008, identified problems with the police service not adopting a corporate approach to IT procurement and stated how mobile IT technology could contribute significantly to reducing police bureaucracy and improving efficiency (Flanagan, 2008, p36).

In January 2009, the NPIA secured a contract with Information Processing Limited to develop a new computerised information system – the Collision Recording and Sharing (CRASH) system – which is to be piloted by the police service early in 2010. The system allows police officers to input collision data directly on to a central (national) system using a mobile device.

REFLECTIVE TASK

Consider how CRASH will reduce bureaucracy and improve efficiency. Make a list of the advantages of using this type of technology for the recording of road collisions. Compare your answers with information provided about the benefits of CRASH on the NPIA website at www.npia.police.uk/en/10513.htm.

Scene capture

The recording of the scene of a road collision will assist in establishing the cause and will also secure potential evidence to assist with an investigation, an inquest and criminal or civil proceedings. Traditional methods of scene capture include a sketch drawn by investigating officers, or in the more serious cases the use of photographs or video and surveying equipment.

Technology now provides even more solutions with the use of laser imaging and GPS mapping that can provide 3D views of the scene. This type of technology will not be used for all traffic collision investigations, but is always a consideration for the roads policing Senior Investigating Officer (SIO) when dealing with fatal or other serious road traffic collisions.

Following a fatal incident, the scene is identified and secured, and all relevant physical material within the scene is recorded. The material is photographed or videoed together with the surrounding topography, and the scene is surveyed to enable the production of a scale plan showing the position of the relevant material. Where possible, aerial photography will be used, involving advanced technologies such as LiDAR (light detection and ranging – laser scanning) that can capture high-resolution imagery of the collision scene.

131

Technology development has led to the reduction of physical evidence at the scene, such as anti-locking brakes, which reduce skid marks (analysis of skid marks can be important in determining speeds of vehicles and road positioning), filamentless xenon gas and LED light sources, which deny filament analysis of light bulbs, and digital tachographs, which reduce opportunities for speed trace data and impact analysis (Labbett, 2008, p3). Further, in-car engine management systems, satellite navigation equipment, and phone technology provide additional challenges to the investigator, presenting problems of data capture, analysis and presentation.

Reducing time in dealing with a road collision is paramount and closure of motorways or major roads at peak periods can create mayhem. The SIO is responsible for managing the disruption and releasing the scene following investigation. Guidance is provided, stating that any closure must be appropriate and proportionate, and that a scene should not be released by the SIO until all expert advice has been taken into consideration and all investigative opportunities have been exploited (NPIA, 2007, p63).

REFLECTIVE TASK

Consider the closure of a motorway or major road during a peak period and write down the implications for road users, business and the public. Then consider the responsibility of the collision investigators and what they are required to achieve during the closure. Having considered the implications, develop an argument either for or against long closures of main arterial roads during peak periods.

You will probably have determined that the implications of a prolonged road closure are severe and that the decision cannot be taken lightly by the police service. Technological solutions are being developed in an attempt to speed up investigation times. For example, in 2008 all police forces in England (except the City of London) were provided with GPS satellite equipment. The technology produces a virtual map of the collision scene, gathers vital evidence and minimises the impact on journey times. Tests found that, on average, a reduction of 5 per cent, or 40 minutes in road closure time, was achieved and in one case as much as 180 minutes (www.highways.gov.uk, 2008).

You may also have considered the possibility of legal ramifications and duty of care issues. Article 2(1) of the Human Rights Act 1998 relates to the right to life that requires effective enforcement of the law, including investigation of all suspicious deaths and the prosecution of alleged offenders. Further, where a person dies in suspicious circumstances, article 13, which relates to the right to an effective remedy, requires a thorough and effective investigation capable of leading to the punishment of those responsible (*Kurt* v. *Turkey* [1998]; *Jordan v. UK* [2001]).

Driving under the influence of drink or drugs

Legislation

The following provides a summary of offences and some of the powers relating to driving while under the influence of alcohol or drugs.

- **Road Traffic Act 1988**: section 1 provides the offence of causing the death of another person while driving a motor vehicle recklessly on a road.

- **Road Traffic Act 1988**: section 3 provides the offence of driving a motor vehicle on a road without due care and attention, or without reasonable consideration for other persons using the road.

- **Road Traffic Act 1988**: section 4 provides the offence of driving or attempting to drive a mechanically propelled vehicle on a road or other public place while unfit to drive through drink or drugs.

- **Road Traffic Act 1988**: section 5 provides the offence of driving, attempting to drive, or being in charge of a motor vehicle on a road or other public place having consumed alcohol, the proportion of which in the blood, breath or urine exceeds the prescribed limit.

- **Railway and Transport Safety Act 2003**: schedule 12 provides the power for a police officer to carry out a preliminary test for drink and drug offences, including an impairment test.

- **Serious Organised Crime Act 2005**: section 154 provides the power for a police officer to carry out an evidential roadside breath test procedure.

A police officer has the power to demand a roadside breath test from the driver of a motor vehicle who has been involved in an accident, who has committed a moving traffic offence or who is suspected of having consumed alcohol. A positive result from a roadside evidential test will end in arrest and a potential charge, whereas a positive result from a roadside screening device will end in arrest, but the driver will undergo further evidential tests at a police station.

Technology used both at the roadside and within the police station is subject to rigorous testing and is type-approved by the Home Office to meet the challenge of evidential scrutiny.

Driving and drugs enforcement

The House of Commons Transport Committee considered the impact of drivers impaired through drugs and highlighted previous research that had revealed the following facts.

- The transport research laboratory provided statistics showing that 18 per cent of drivers involved in collisions between 1996 and 1999 had taken illegal substances, compared with only 3 per cent between 1985 and 1987.

- During the 1980s, the number of people killed or seriously injured in drink-drive collisions reduced from about 9,000 to just under 5,000. However, in the previous decade (prior to 2006), numbers had fluctuated but no improvement had been seen.

- During the previous five years (prior to 2006), laboratory tests for drugs following a driving-related incident increased from 350 to 3,700 per year.

(adapted from House of Commons, 2006, pp47 and 49)

The report clearly recognised the increasing impact of drivers who were impaired by drugs and the apparent inability of the police service to effectively deal with this type of offence. There was evidence that technology was available to assist the police in carrying out roadside drug tests, but problems had been identified with development and funding and, as a result, the equipment was not being made available to police officers. The report urged the Home Office to give the development of drug-screening equipment some priority and make it available for use at the earliest opportunity.

A police officer can ask a driver who is suspected of driving under the influence of drugs to take a 'field impairment test' (the driver is asked to complete five tests that may provide the officer with evidence of impairment). However, field tests completed by researchers from Glasgow University highlighted problems with judgements being made by police officers about impairment (Oliver et al., 2006, p30). Technological development is clearly necessary and urgently required, but is complex in relation to designing a device that can detect the many drugs currently available.

REFLECTIVE TASK

The House of Commons Transport Committee published their eleventh report in 2008, in which a further recommendation was made relating to the introduction of drug-screening equipment. A response was provided by the government on 19 January 2009.

Read through the response at www.publications.parliament.uk/pa/cm200809/cmselect/ cmtran/136/13604.htm and consider whether the delays are acceptable for such an important piece of technology being made readily available to operational police officers.

A parliamentary briefing paper (standard note) is also available that provides more detail in respect of the parliamentary reply given on 19/1/09: www.parliament.uk/commons/lib/ research/briefings/snbt-02884.pdf.

Alcohol ignition interlocks

Section 15 of the Road Safety Act 2006 allows a court to offer an alcohol ignition interlock programme order to persons convicted of drink-drive offences who meet certain criteria provided by the Act. During the period of the order, the offender's vehicle will be fitted with a type-approved breath-testing device and any result containing over 9 micro-grammes of alcohol in 100 millilitres of breath will cause the vehicle ignition to remain locked. The programme includes a rehabilitative course, with the cost of both the course and the fitting of the device being met by the offender. The programme is subject to an experimental period to be completed by the end of 2010.

Alcohol ignition locks are successfully used in other countries such as North America, Australia and Sweden for recidivist drink-drive offenders and as a deterrent for drivers of fleet transport and public service vehicles. The technology has excellent potential to contribute to road safety and cut the incidents of drink-driving and, in the future, we may well see all new vehicles being fitted with the devices.

CHAPTER SUMMARY

Within this chapter you have been provided with an overview of some of the cutting-edge technology that is now available to the police service and other organisations to make the roads of the UK safer. We have seen how effective roads policing can have an impact on crime by denying criminals the use of the road.

Opportunities have been provided for further research and a number of contemporaneous issues have been considered, such as privacy, balance between police officers and technology, safety camera concerns, and road closures.

The tasks completed should provide stimulus, sources and evidence for completion of NOS and assignments. Further reading and research will provide a more detailed understanding of the impact of technology on policing and how it is shaping road safety strategy.

Association of Chief Police Officers (ACPO) (2004) *E.C.H.R. Data Protection & RIPA Guidance Relating to the Police Use of A.N.P.R.* London: ACPO National ANPR User Group.

Association of Chief Police Officers (ACPO) (2005) *ANPR Strategy for the Police Service 2005/2008: Denying criminals the use of the road.* London: ACPO ANPR Steering Group.

Association of Chief Police Officers (ACPO) (2007) *Practice Advice on the Policing of Roads.* Wyboston: National Policing Improvement Agency.

Carston, Oliver and Fowkes, Mark (2000) *External Vehicle Speed Control: Executive summary of project results.* Leeds: Institute for Transport Studies. Available online at www.its.leeds.ac.uk/projects/evsc/exec3.pdf (accessed 6 September 2009).

Community Justice Portal (2002) Driving crime off the roads: automatic number plate recognition systems launched nationwide. Available online at www.cjp.org.uk/news/archive/driving-crime-off-the-roads-automatic-number-plate-recognition-systems-launched-nationwide-14-11-200 (accessed 3 July 2009).

Department for Transport (DfT) (2009a) *Road Casualties in Great Britain: Main results 2008.* Available online at www.dft.gov.uk/pgr/statistics/datatablespublications/accidents/casualtiesmr/rcgbmainresults2008 (accessed 25 June 2009).

Department for Transport (DfT) (2009b) *Safety Cameras – Frequently Asked Questions: What is the history of safety cameras?* Available online at www.dft.gov.uk/pgr/roadsafety/speedmanagement/safetycamerasfrequentlyasked4603?page=1#a1013 (accessed 1 July 2009).

Department for Transport (DfT) (2009c) *Road Safety Cameras.* Available online at www.dft.gov.uk/pgr/roadsafety/speedmanagement/roadsafetycameras (accessed 1 July 2009).

Driver and Vehicle Licensing Agency (DVLA) (2009) DVLA driver and vehicle statistics. Available online at: www.dvla.gov.uk/pressoffice/stats.aspx?keywords=statistics (accessed 25 June 2009).

Flanagan, Sir Ronnie (2008) *The Review of Policing: Final report.* London: Home Office.

Her Majesty's Inspectorate of Constabulary (HMIC) (1998) *Road Policing and Traffic.* London: Home Office.

Hicks, Joe and Allen, Grahame (1999) *A Century of Change: Trends in UK statistics since 1900*, House of Commons research paper 99/111. London: House of Commons Library.

Home Office (2003) *Automatic Number Plate Recognition (ANPR)*, Police Standards Unit (PSU) news sheet 26. London: Home Office.

House of Commons Transport Committee (2005) *Traffic Policing and Technology: Getting the balance right*, press notice. London: House of Commons. Available online at www.parliament.uk/parliamentary_committees/transport_committee/trans05_06_press_notice22.cfm (accessed 29 June 2009).

House of Commons Transport Committee (2006) *Roads Policing and Technology: Getting the balance right: Tenth report of session 2005–06*: London: The Stationery Office.

Labbett, Simon (2008) *Developing the Role of Collision Investigation*, Road Peace. Available online at www.roadpeace.org/documents/Simon%20Labett%20Developing%20the%20role%20of%20collision%20investigation2.PDF (accessed 9 July 2009).

Livingstone, Ken (2002) *Cleaning London's Air: Highlights of the Mayor's air quality strategy.* London: Greater London Authority.

National Policing Improvement Agency (NPIA) (2007) *Road Death Investigation Manual*. Wyboston: NPIA.

Office for National Statistics (ONS) (2009) *Accidental Deaths: By cause 1971–1998*, Social Trends 31. Available online at www.statistics.gov.uk/STATBASE/ssdataset.asp?vlnk=3546 (accessed 25 June 2009).

Oliver, J S, Seymour, A, Wylie, F M, Torrance, H and Anderson, R A (2006) *Monitoring the Effectiveness of UK Field Impairment Tests*, Road safety research report No. 63. London: Department for Transport.

PA Consulting Group (2005) *Denying Criminals the Use of the Roads through 'Joined up' Application of Number Plate Recognition Technology*. London: PA Consulting Knowledge.

PA Consulting Group (2007) *Police Standards Unit: Evaluation of automatic number plate recognition 2006/07*. London: PA Consulting Knowledge.

Ward, Heather (2003) *The History and Development of Speed Camera Use in Great Britain: A report to Monash University Accident Research Centre.* London: Centre for Transport Studies. Available online at http://eprints.ucl.ac.uk/2028/1/2003_50.pdf (accessed 1 July 2009).

www.highways.gov.uk (2008) *Project Milestone: Collision investigation equipment*. Available online at www.highways.gov.uk/business/18040.aspx (accessed 9 July 2009).

www.publictechnology.net (2007) Automatic Number Plate Recognition technology cuts Manchester crime, 29 November. Available online at www.publictechnology.net/modules.php?op=modload&name=News&file=article&sid=12977 (accessed 8 July 2009).

www.thisistotalessex.co.uk (2008) Speeding motorists in Dunmow tracked by police helicopter, 28 August. Available online at www.thisistotalessex.co.uk/dunmow/Speeding-motorists-Dunmow-tracked-police-helicopter/article-292657-detail/article.html (accessed 1 July 2009).

USEFUL WEBSITES

www.crimereduction.homeoffice.gov.uk (Home Office's Crime Reduction website)

www.dft.gov.uk (Department for Transport)

www.dvla.gov.uk (Driver and Vehicle Licensing Agency)

www.highways.gov.uk (Highways Agency)

www.homeoffice.gov.uk (Home Office, with links to crime information, the police and statistics)

www.parliament.co.uk (UK Parliament, with links to legislation and other topics of interest)

www.vosa.gov.uk (Vehicle & Operator Services Agency)

CASES

Jordan v. *UK* [2001] 37 EHRR 52

Kurt v. *Turkey* [1998] 27 EHRR 373 or 5 BHRC 1

LEGISLATION

Human Rights Act 1998

Railway and Transport Safety Act 2003

Road Safety Act 2006

Road Traffic Act 1988

Road Traffic Act 1991

Road Traffic Offenders Act 1988

Road Traffic Regulations Act 1984

Serious Organised Crime Act 2005

Vehicle (Crimes) Act 2001

9 Communications and custody

CHAPTER OBJECTIVES

By the end of this chapter you should be able to:

- outline the development and application of technology within police communications;
- describe the development and application of technology within the police custody area;
- analyse a number of key issues relating to police communications and technology;
- discuss a number of key issues relating to the use of technologies within the police custody area.

LINKS TO STANDARDS

This chapter provides opportunities for links with the following Skills for Justice, National Occupational Standards (NOS) for Policing and Law Enforcement 2008.

AE1   Maintain and develop your own knowledge, skills and competence.
CD1   Provide an initial response to an incident.
CI101   Conduct priority and volume investigations.
CJ101   Interview victims and witnesses in relation to priority and volume investigations.
CJ201   Interview suspects in relation to priority and volume investigations.
FA102   Present detained persons to custody.
HA1   Manage your own resources.
HA2   Manage your own resources and professional development.

Introduction

This chapter is divided into two sections. First, we explore the development of police communications, and the impact of technology and how it has enhanced investigative opportunities. Second, we discover how technology has been developed and utilised within the custody (detention) area of a police station to provide safeguards and how this, too, has enhanced the investigative process.

Police communications

Communication is the 'lifeblood' of any organisation and the modern police service is no exception. For over a century, telecommunications have played an important role in providing an effective and responsive police service. The public need to communicate with the police quickly, easily and at any time to report emergencies, incidents and crimes. Technology has developed considerably from early cumbersome telegraph systems and telephones to sophisticated mobile devices and expansive call centre technology. Millions of electronic communications are made on a daily basis and are recorded in many forms that can be accessed by the discerning investigator.

In this section, we will highlight some of the technology that is used to facilitate and effectively manage communications with both the general public and operational police officers. We will also identify how some of the technology can be exploited to provide invaluable investigative and intelligence opportunities for the police service.

The technology that will be explored and discussed is:

- call handling and deployment (command and control);
- the Police National Computer (PNC);
- Airwave (radio system);
- crime reporting;
- mobile data devices;
- crime mapping.

Historical perspective

In 1829, Sir Robert Peel founded the modern police service and at this time effective communication technology did not exist. Patrolling officers had to rely on a loud shout or use of a whistle to communicate with each other. Prior to 1900, a number of communication devices such as the telegraph, telephone, radio and teletypewriter became available. The telephone was introduced to society by Alexander Graham Bell, who patented his invention in 1876. By the turn of the twentieth century, police pillar boxes that contained a telephone were being introduced into some of the major cities in Britain for use by both police officers and certain members of the general public to make contact with the emergency services.

During the 1930s, the police service adopted a new standardised General Post Office Police Signal Box System, easily recognisable today as the 'Tardis' used in the BBC's *Doctor Who* series. One of the largest networks of this type of signal box could be found in Glasgow, where 323 signal boxes were introduced in a six-year period from 1932. The signal boxes were equipped with a flashing light that was used to alert the patrolling constable that a member of the public required assistance, or that divisional headquarters wanted to make contact (Stewart, 1994).

At the time of introducing the signal boxes, and for many years thereafter, most people did not have a private telephone, so the signal boxes, together with public telephone kiosks, were a vital means of communication with the emergency services.

As technology developed and telephone access and ownership became more widely available to the general public, the signal boxes were no longer required. The police service developed information rooms that received emergency and routine telephone calls from members of the public, and dispatched officers to the scene of the incident or referred the call to other emergency services.

REFLECTIVE TASK

Consider the ways in which a member of the public can now make contact with the police through the use of technology. Make a list of the methods available and consider the impact that technology has had on modern-day policing and what opportunities it may provide for an investigator.

The introduction of satellite technology has had a major impact on policing. Large numbers of people now own a mobile telephone and have immediate access to the emergency services. The use of the Internet is now commonplace and this has provided the public with a wider range of communication mechanisms to make contact with the police. The younger generation are more likely to use the Internet and mobile texting as a means of communication, and there are some good examples of the police making the best use of opportunities provided by the Internet by utilising applications such as 'Twitter', 'Flickr' or 'YouTube', and using RSS feeds and podcasts to provide information.

Most police organisations have a website that provides a range of contact details and informs the public how to report emergencies, crimes and incidents. These sites are also used to make contact with local neighbourhood teams or other policing teams, and they provide links to other organisations that can assist the police with investigations, such as Crimestoppers.

PRACTICAL TASK

- *Go to the Metropolitan Police website at www.met.police.uk and discover the range of ways in which contact can be made with them.*

- *You will find a link to 'Flickr' towards the bottom of the homepage – click on the link and see how the Metropolitan Police use Flickr to display stolen property and invite information from members of the public.*

- *Consider accessing the websites of other police organisations and compare their communication methods with those on the Metropolitan Police website.*

The explosion in and availability of communications technology has caused severe problems for the police, such as the huge increase in the number of calls being made to them that have to be recorded and dealt with. For example, between 1996/97 and 2000/01, 999 calls to the police increased by 33 per cent, which could be attributed to the growth in mobile phone ownership. One early incident highlighted the growing problem when 91 calls were received reporting a swan loose on the M25 motorway (Povey, 2001, p135). Currently, the police service deals with about 80 million telephone calls a year (Home Office, 2009a).

The increase in calls and introduction of more effective means of communication have resulted in the growth and collection of vast amounts of information. The police have had to respond to the challenges provided by new technology and, although some of the challenges have been profound, technology has provided the police with new investigative opportunities, and the smart modern investigator will embrace the opportunities provided.

Call handling and deployment

The modern police communications centre is supported by sophisticated command-and-control technology to effectively manage interaction with the public, logging of calls, allocation of resources, and support to operational officers by providing access to key information that enables them to respond appropriately to the calls received.

The command-and-control system needs to be available 24 hours a day, 365 days a year. Emergencies can be reported at any time and lives will depend on services being available in the right place at the right time. It is important that operational officers are provided with information that is up to date and accurate, so that they can respond to incidents quickly, safely and effectively.

Command-and-control systems can interact with other IT applications, providing links to a variety of specialist services that enable and enhance operational, investigative and intelligence capabilities. An officer can be provided with an extensive range of information before, during and after any incident responded to. Examples of what information the system can provide include:

- details of previous incidents linked to the address or location;

- any known dangers or hazards;

- names of persons linked with an address or location;

- warnings of firearms, drugs, weapons or violence;

- any known mental health or welfare issues;

- detailed geographical mapping to direct officers to a location quickly;

- easy access to emergency procedures for firearms incidents, chemical spills, train crashes or disasters;

- the location of resources to enable quickest deployment.

The system also provides essential links to specialist departments, such as child protection, hate crime or domestic violence units, which can be notified immediately of relevant incidents and take appropriate action to improve efficiency and the service provided to victims.

Call handling

It is important that the public have the confidence in the police to report incidents and provide information that can be used not only for dealing with the incident reported, but also to assist an investigator:

> The majority of the public make their initial contact with the police through the telephony system, and first impressions count. It is vital that 21st century technology is employed to provide the public with swift and easy access to police services.
>
> (Povey, 2001, p154)

An effective interface between members of the public and the police service is critical and the first point of contact is very often a telephone call reporting an incident that has to be dealt with by the police call taker. When a call is received there are four distinct processes:

- the initial contact;

- an assessment of the incident (urgent/non-urgent/deployment of officer required?);

- secondary-level call handling – resolving the call without deployment of an officer;

- dispatching an officer to the incident.

> (adapted from Povey, 2001, p134)

The modern police call centre is dependent on technology to receive and manage calls, and the above processes will be incorporated into command-and-control systems to record the information received, actions taken and results achieved.

REFLECTIVE TASK

Consider how the information obtained and actions taken by call centre staff could be of use to an investigator

---

When investigating a crime, it is important always to check the initial incident log, which may contain details of witnesses, a description or name of a suspect, and other information that may provide lines of enquiry. Some of the information provided may be critical and certain action may need to be taken for evidential purposes. For example, the incident log will have to be disclosed if a person is charged with a criminal offence (Criminal Procedure and Investigations Act 1996) and, if identification is an issue, the incident log may contain the 'first description' of a suspect that is required for identification procedures (Police and Criminal Evidence Act 1984 – Codes of Practice D3.1).

Modern call centres will also record all telephone conversations, which will provide another line of enquiry for the investigator. For example, there are cases where an offender will report a crime anonymously and the recording and its source may lead the investigator directly to the perpetrator.

Police National Computer

The Police National Computer (PNC) was first introduced in 1974 as a single vehicle database. Since this time, it has been considerably developed and now offers a comprehensive online intelligence and investigatory tool. It incorporates a number of databases, including:

- names;
- vehicles;
- drivers;
- property.

Staff within police communications centres will have access to the PNC to provide operational officers with important information while on patrol, such as details of stolen vehicles, the registered keeper of a vehicle, wanted and missing persons, descriptions, previous convictions, warnings, disqualified drivers, and identification of property. Recent developments have seen the application integrated with ANPR (see Chapter 8) and mobile data devices (see below), giving the operational police officer even speedier access to information. Links have also been made with databases from other agencies – for example, a police officer can quickly establish whether a motor vehicle is insured or has a current test certificate.

The investigative capability of the PNC is well recognised by the police investigator and can be used in a number of different ways to assist in the identification of a suspect, vehicle or property. The following are good examples.

- **Querying Using Enhanced or Extended Search Techniques (QUEST)**: This tool allows an investigator to carry out searches on the names database in cases where there is limited information about a suspect, such as a part description or nickname.

- **Vehicle Online Descriptive Search (VODS)**: This can be used to identify a vehicle if only part of a VRN is taken or a witness has made a slight error in recording it. In cases where the make of a vehicle only is known, but it is believed to be a local vehicle, a postcode search could quickly identify the vehicle concerned.

- **CRIMELINK**: This provides the opportunity for crime and intelligence analysts to access the PNC databases to identify national patterns and links that can assist with the identification and conviction of suspects.

Airwave

Airwave provides a digital radio service for the police, fire and ambulance services. It has replaced analogue radio, which was becoming unreliable, and, according to the NPIA (2009a), has provided the police service with a number of benefits:

- an emergency button that an officer can press if in danger;

- improved radio coverage;

- improved speech clarity;

- improved security and encryption of communications;

- enhanced operational flexibility;

- scope for mobile data applications;

- national roaming;

- improved capability for radio interoperability between police forces and other emergency services.

Crime reporting

Thousands of criminal offences are committed on a daily basis and one of the key roles of the police service is to reduce and detect crime. The public need confidence in the police in order to report crime, and the police need crime to be reported to bring offenders to justice, reduce crime and improve safety within the community.

Confidence in the police to investigate crime is important and effective communication is paramount to ensure that crime is reported. Any victim of crime should be able to report a crime easily, and will have expectations of an appropriate response, a police service that takes an interest in the crime committed, and confidence that an appropriate investigation will take place.

Today there are a number of ways in which a person can report a crime, including:

- telephone – 999 or direct line, usually to a helpdesk at a police station;

- personal visit to a police station;

- letter to a police station;

- direct to a police officer;

- via a police website on the Internet;

- anonymously by telephone, for example to an organisation such as Crimestoppers;

- via an intermediary, for example a solicitor;

- via a support agency, for example Childline;

- by telephone or the Internet direct to a non-police investigating agency that deals with, for example, benefit fraud, tax evasion, credit card fraud, telephone scams, etc.

The biggest innovation for contemporary policing has been the introduction of web-based technology that has provided new and improved methods of communication including opportunities to report crime. However, it should be noted that there are restrictions on the types of crime that can be reported online. For example, the Metropolitan Police (2009) clearly stipulate that only the following crimes can be reported online:

- theft – excluding robbery and burglary;

- criminal damage;

- theft from a motor vehicle;

- criminal damage to a motor vehicle;

- hate crimes and hate incidents.

REFLECTIVE TASK

Consider the use of the Internet as a means of reporting crime and what impact this may have on public confidence about the ability of the police to investigate crime effectively.

Crime has grown considerably, for example 1,555,995 crimes were recorded by the police in 1970, compared to 4,703,814 in the year 2008/09 (Home Office, 2009b). We have already seen (pages 140–1) how the number of incidents reported to the police has increased considerably. Prior to these increases, the policy of the police service was to provide, where possible, a personal service to members of the public, no matter what type of crime was being reported. A victim could expect an early visit from the police following the report of a crime, and both a witness statement and crime complaint would be completed. The investigating officer was also responsible for further visits to the victim to provide updates or the results of the investigation.

As both crime and the number of incidents reported to the police increased, it became apparent that the police service could no longer provide the same level of service. Senior officers had to make some difficult decisions to ensure that police resources were effectively deployed to meet increasing demands in relation not only to crimes and incidents, but also to other issues such as serious organised crime and the growing threat of terrorism.

Sir Ronnie Flanagan carried out a review of policing in 2007 and in his final report he recognised the need to tackle police bureaucracy to free up officer time. He made a number of recommendations, including the use of standard IT systems and mobile devices across the police service (rec. 10), and to streamline the crime recording process (rec. 21) (Flanagan, 2008).

A further government report, *From the Neighbourhood to the National*, published in July 2008, recognised the recommendations made by Sir Ronnie Flanagan and, as part of the solution to free up officer time, the government made a commitment to provide additional funding for 30,000 extra mobile devices to be in the hands of frontline police officers by March 2010 (Home Office, 2008, p42).

Mobile data devices

The use of mobile data devices allows the operational police officer to complete a number of functions that would ordinarily have required a return to the police station for form filling or other investigative enquiries. It also means that an officer is able to spend more time on patrol, thus increasing police visibility and enhancing public reassurance. Examples of tasks that an officer can complete with a mobile data device include:

- a search of national and local databases to provide real-time information that may be useful when checking a person or vehicle on patrol;

- access to briefings, including photographs, to identify people of interest and those who are wanted, missing or vulnerable;

- receiving and updating tasks or incident reports;

- completion of police forms, such as stop and search accounts and crime reports. (This can prevent double keying of information and provide real-time information to assist investigators.)

(adapted from Home Office, 2008, p43)

PRACTICAL TASK

Carry out some research on the Internet and find out how the police service is adapting to the use of mobile data devices. Establish what benefits are being achieved and whether there is any evidence of improved police efficiency, public confidence and customer service. For example, visit the NPIA website and find out about the 'Mobile Information Programme', or complete a Google or Bing search using the phrase: 'Police mobile data East Midlands'.

Crime mapping

We will complete this section by briefly considering the use of 'crime mapping' as a means of communication. In January 2009, ACPO published a *Policing Pledge*, which provided a list of minimum standards that the public can expect from the police service. The pledge included the following promise:

> *[To] provide monthly updates on progress, and on local crime and policing issues. This will include the provision of crime maps, information on specific crimes and what happened to those brought to justice, details of what action we and our partners are taking to make your neighbourhood safer and information on how your force is performing.*

(Directgov, 2009)

The power of Internet technology and the use of digital maps have assisted with the delivery of the above pledge. The NPIA has provided a 'Local crime mapping' website (http://maps.police.uk), which provides information on crime and antisocial behaviour wherever you live in England or Wales. The government also provide a section on their website (www.direct.gov.uk) that gives direct access to crime maps, together with other information and links to local policing teams, the probation service, courts and victim support groups.

Crime mapping for Scotland and Northern Ireland can be found at www.sns.gov.uk and www.ninis.nisra.gov.uk/mapxtreme/default.asp respectively.

Police custody

We shall now explore how technology has been developed and used in a police custody suite, where a person is taken to following an arrest. While in custody a person can be searched, interviewed and detained in a cell or detention room until charged, bailed or released without charge.

Early custody suites were bleak places where suspects were processed by the police with little accountability. The public did not have a general right of access to the custody suite and had limited knowledge of what actually took place within the reception area, cells, charge office or interview room.

We will discover how certain events and subsequent legislation provided safeguards for those entering police custody and how the police service has become more accountable, with the introduction of technological devices such as electronic custody records, tape and video recording of interviews, and CCTV surveillance. We will also consider briefly the development and use of technological solutions for identifying suspects on video identification parades and explore technology used for fingerprinting and obtaining footwear impressions.

Historical perspective

One key piece of legislation to consider is the Police and Criminal Evidence Act (PACE) 1984, which was introduced on 1 January 1986 and provides a range of safeguards for persons arrested, interviewed and detained in police custody. Prior to PACE, there had been considerable public disquiet about police powers and a number of well-publicised events led to a Royal Commission on Criminal Procedure (RCCP) between 1978 and 1981, whose recommendations resulted in the introduction of PACE.

Before the Act, police powers were governed by common law, statute and, most controversially, the Judges' Rules, which were introduced in 1912 to provide the police with judicial guidance for the detention and questioning of suspects. These rules could easily be flouted and, following a series of miscarriages of justice, they were brought into disrepute.

The catalyst for change was the murder of Maxwell Confait in Lewisham, London, in April 1972. Three youths were arrested for the offence; one was aged 14, the second was aged 15 and had a very low IQ, and the third was aged 18 with a mental age of 8. All were interviewed without an adult being present and, at the later trial, claimed that confessions were only made because of police brutality. All were convicted but, following a long campaign, the case went to the Court of Appeal in 1975. The Court overturned the convictions and the three were released from prison. In November of the same year, the government announced an enquiry into the investigation and appointed Sir Henry Fisher as chair whose report was published in December 1977. Sir Henry suggested that a Royal Commission should be set up to look at the issue of police investigations and, the following year, the RCCP was announced by the government.

The RCCP reported in 1981 and recommended an overhaul of the criminal investigative process. It highlighted the need to maintain a balance between the powers and duties of the police and the rights and duties of suspects. PACE was the direct result and a statutory framework was provided for the criminal investigation process. The Judges' Rules were abolished and PACE codes of practice were published that clearly stated the rights of an individual and the powers of the police for certain key areas of procedure (Home Office, 2009c). There are currently eight codes of practice:

- Code A: Stop and search;

- Code B: Searching of premises and seizure of property;

- Code C: Detention treatment and questioning;

- Code D: Identification;

- Code E: Audio recording of interviews with suspects;

- Code F: Visual recording of interviews;

- Code G: Power of arrest;

- Code H: Detention, questioning and treatment of terrorist suspects.

You will probably have considered how the use of technology such as automated custody records, CCTV and audio recording is an essential component of a modern custody suite. PACE requires that a log (custody record) is kept of all actions taken while a person is in police custody (PACE, Code C2), and sections 60 and 60A of PACE introduced powers and the requirement for audio and visual interview of suspects. It is also a possibility that a suspect may complain about the way he or she has been treated in custody and, more seriously, deaths in custody do occur, so the use of CCTV within the custody suite can be critical to any subsequent investigation. CCTV images can contribute to the protection of those who work within the custody suite, such as in countering false allegations and by providing some reassurance to the community, whose suspicions of police malpractice may be allayed by CCTV evidence. We shall now consider some of this technology in more detail and its use within police custody suites.

Electronic custody record

When a person is arrested and taken to a police custody suite, they will be presented to a custody officer who is required to be of at least the rank of Sergeant (PACE, s36(3)). The custody officer will be appropriately trained and has a number of key responsibilities to ensure that the detained person is dealt with in accordance with the law and PACE codes of practice. Upon arrival of a suspect at the custody suite, the custody officer will commence a custody record that will record important information relating to the detention and also provide an account of any actions and decisions taken during the detention period. The following list provides some examples of what information may be found on a custody record:

- time, date, place of arrest and arresting officer;

- grounds for arrest and authorisation to detain in custody;

- reason for detention, for example to secure evidence or obtain evidence by questioning;

- personal details and a description of the detainee;

- a list of property found in possession of the detainee;

- record of any injuries, illness or intoxication;

- record that detainee has been provided with statutory rights, for example to have a nominated person informed of detention, access to a solicitor, and access to a copy of the PACE codes of practice;

- details of persons given access to or supporting the detainee, such as a doctor, an appropriate adult, or a solicitor;

- record of all visits made to the cell;

- record of times the detainee is handed over for interview;

- record of certain authorisations required by law, such as an inspector's authority to obtain an intimate sample (PACE, s62);

- timings of PACE reviews and a recording of any representations made by the detainee or solicitor;

- bail conditions;

- time of charge and/or release.

The police service now uses electronic custody records that are far more efficient and reliable than the earlier handwritten ones. The manual completion of custody records was time-consuming, and the accuracy of recorded timings could be problematic, particularly where a custody record had been completed retrospectively. One of the latest innovations for the custody suite is the introduction of a 'Custody and case preparation' application that is able to link the custody record with the building of the case file to avoid double-keying of information. The custody record is also linked to the PNC, which can be updated in real time to record details such as court appearances and bail conditions (NPIA, 2009c).

For any investigation relating to the arrest and detention of a person in police custody, it is essential that the custody record is secured for examination and scrutiny by the investigation team, respective legal representatives, and the court where appropriate.

CCTV surveillance

CCTV surveillance within a custody suite is now common practice and provides the investigator with another means of obtaining information and potential evidence following a complaint or death in custody. It can also provide good corroborative evidence for a police officer, such as the finding and recovery of stolen property or drugs during a custody search, or capturing a significant statement made by the detainee that could be used in evidence.

The importance of CCTV was recognised following a series of high-profile deaths in police custody during the 1970s, which raised concerns about police violence and the treatment and welfare of people detained at police stations.

CASE STUDY

Liddle Towers was a 39-year-old electrician with no history of violence who died on 9 February 1977 in hospital from injuries received at the hands of police officers during the early hours of 16 January 1976. He was arrested outside a nightclub and, after a struggle, he was put into a dog van by six police officers and taken to Gateshead police station, Northumbria. He complained of feeling unwell and was taken to hospital where, following an examination, there were allegedly no injuries or illness found. He was taken back to the police station and released from custody later the same day. Following his release, Towers informed a friend and his local GP that he had been assaulted by the police both upon arrest and in the cells at Gateshead police station. At the later inquest, the coroner returned a verdict of 'justifiable homicide' (Radice, 1977). Following an intervention by the Attorney General, a second inquest delivered a verdict of 'death by misadventure'.

Liddle Towers' death was one of a series involving the police both in custody suites and in other situations, such as on arrest. The media, human rights groups and relatives and friends of the deceased campaigned to obtain justice for their loved ones. In particular, concern was being raised by ethnic minority groups about the level of police violence and the disproportionality of black, minority and ethnic group deaths in police custody.

Following the death of Blair Peach in 1979, two members of Parliament, Michael Meacher and Stan Newens, raised questions about the number of, and causes of, deaths while in the custody of the police. Research found that 274 people had died in police custody between 1970 and 1979 and, as a result, in 1980 the Home Affairs Select Committee of the House of Commons considered the problem of deaths in police custody. They reported that they had found no evidence of generalised police brutality against those in custody (Newburn and Hayman, 2002, pp5–6).

As previously highlighted, this and other factors contributed to a lack of confidence in the criminal justice system that resulted in the RCCP and the introduction of PACE, providing new safeguards for the arrest, questioning and detention of suspects.

Despite the new safeguards, deaths in police custody or following police contact continued at an alarming rate and, some years later, the following comment was made in a report provided by the support group Inquest to the Stephen Lawrence Inquiry:

> *The disproportionate number of individuals, particularly Africans and African-Caribbeans, who have died in suspicious circumstances in police custody has reinforced the idea that many of these deaths are a reflection of racism within the police and are as a result of racially-motivated brutality.*

(Inquest, 1998, p1)

In 1998, the Home Office published a research paper that presented findings from the study of official records relating to 277 deaths in police custody between 1990 and 1996. The purpose of the study was to establish what lessons could be learned to help prevent future deaths. At this time, the use of CCTV within custody suites was not widespread and only 23 CCTV cameras were in use for the cases examined. The issue of using CCTV within cells was considered and the following observations were made based on the research completed.

- The case for CCTV is more complex than appears at first.

- CCTV in itself does not eliminate risk.

- CCTV does not remove the need to physically check detainees.

- CCTV does not guarantee that everything that happens will be noted by custody staff.

- CCTV can be of benefit for early detection of medical collapse or self-harm.

- The cost of CCTV may be prohibitive.

- The positioning of CCTV cameras could cause privacy issues.

(adapted from Leigh et al., 2008, pp82–3)

In 1999, further academic research was completed when CCTV cameras were introduced to the custody suite at Kilburn police station, North London. Cameras were installed to provide cover of the reception area, cell corridors and all cells. The purpose of the research was to view the nature and impact of the use of the technology and to bring into focus new questions and issues of the use of surveillance in a new environment. The research provided more useful findings and recommendations.

- Custody staff should be properly trained and be aware of agreed protocols.

- There was a need for evidential integrity with the removal and storage of tapes.

- CCTV coverage should be extended to cover areas such as the room where breath testing is carried out and the property store.

- CCTV provided additional protection for the removal and seizure of detainees' property.

- Detainees should be informed of the presence of cameras.

- There was a need to consider whether the system should be open or closed; for example, an open system allows a detainee to be constantly monitored by custody staff but has privacy implications.

- All cells should have CCTV cameras.

- The toilet area should be electronically masked from the monitoring screen.

- Protocols should be developed to provide minimum standards for camera monitoring and should be made available to the public.

- Strip searches should be monitored using closed CCTV surveillance.

- Plexiglas booths should be installed to allow private communication with solicitors.

(adapted from Newburn and Hayman, 2002, pp171–8)

REFLECTIVE TASK

Consider the findings of the research highlighted above and how it might contribute to allaying fears and improving confidence within communities about police actions within a custody suite.

The use of CCTV surveillance within police custody areas is now commonplace and is providing additional safeguards for custody suite staff, suspects and visitors. Following the introduction of the Police Reform Act 2002, the police service is required to report any deaths following police contact to the Independent Police Complaints Commission (IPCC) for investigation. The IPCC reported that, in 2008/09, 92 deaths were referred to them, 15 of which were deaths in or following police custody, with only two of the 15 deaths occurring in a police cell (IPCC, 2009).

PRACTICAL TASK

Go to www.suffolk.police.uk/NR/rdonlyres/BF253A19-231C-478F-8B5E-DE51270D766A/0/ CustodyCCTV.pdf, read through Suffolk Constabulary's Custody – CCTV procedures, and compare them with the recommendations made in the Kilburn research highlighted above. Identify which of the recommendations have been adopted as well as other safeguards that have been introduced in Suffolk.

Investigative interviewing

This is another very controversial area of policing that contributed to the major changes within the criminal justice system during the 1980s following a series of miscarriages of justice. Police interviewing practice prior to PACE was confession-based rather than a search for the truth. This became more apparent in high-profile cases in which the police were under pressure to get a speedy result and where unethical methods were used in some cases to obtain a confession.

CASE STUDY

On 19 September 1978, 13-year-old Carl Bridgewater was shot at point blank range while delivering a newspaper to a farmhouse in South Staffordshire. It is believed that he had disturbed a number of men who were in the process of committing a burglary. Following a substantial police enquiry, four men from the West Midlands were arrested and two confessions were obtained. There were no witnesses to the crime and no forensic evidence to support the confessions made, and the four men were convicted on confessional evidence alone.

Following many years of protesting their innocence and a high-profile media campaign, three of the men were released by the Court of Appeal on 22 February 1997. The fourth man, Patrick Molloy, died in prison during 1981. It was proved through the use of modern forensic technology (electrostatic definition analysis – ESDA) that one of the written confessions had been forged. It was also alleged, but not conclusively proved, that Molloy was assaulted while being questioned, had salt put in his food, was refused liquids and was deprived of sleep. Michael Mansfield QC later referred to the vine of corruption and dishonesty that ran through the whole case (Regan, 1997). At the time of the arrest of these men, police interviews were not electronically recorded.

Tape recording

Section 60 of PACE provided for the tape recording of interviews with persons detained at a police station on suspicion of the commission of a criminal offence. In 1984, field trials were carried out in six police areas (Leicester, the Wirral, Winchester, South Shields/Jarrow, Croydon and Holburn) to test and develop the use of tape recording for interviewing suspects.

REFLECTIVE TASK

Consider what impact the introduction of the tape recording of suspect interviews might have had at this time and make a list of some of the issues that you think it may have raised. Consider impacts on the suspect, the police service and the general public.

You may have highlighted issues such as training, cost, suitability of equipment, evidential integrity, potential for reduction in confessions made, and increased public confidence. The Home Office provided two reports following the field trials: the first in 1984, where it was found that tape recording did not inhibit suspects from confessing (Willis, 1984, p32); and the second in 1988, which provided further findings, including:

- a reduction in the length of interviews;
- a saving of officers' time in writing up notes on interviews;
- surprisingly, in two of the field trials, an increase in confessions;
- the faster release of suspects not charged with an offence;
- very few occasions when a suspect objected to being tape recorded;
- the disadvantage of having to occasionally transcribe the recordings;
- that some officers continued to believe that in some cases tape recording impeded procurement of a confession and other information during interview.

(adapted from Willis et al., 1988, pp73–6)

The use of the tape recording of suspects was adopted throughout the police service. Prior to the field trials, there was little knowledge of what actually happened in a police interview room, and now both lawyers and researchers had the benefit of finding out what was taking place, enabling evaluation and scrutiny of both evidential issues and police performance.

REFLECTIVE TASK

Debate and argue whether you consider the safeguards introduced by the tape recording of suspects in police custody has prevented false confessions by suspects.

You will probably have thought that the fact interviews could be listened to would in itself prevent any miscarriage of justice; however, two cases are worthy of note and show that the tape recording of police interviews is by no means foolproof.

CASE STUDY

R v. Paris, Abdullahi and Miller [1992]

The accused in this case were arrested, charged and convicted of the murder of Lynette White in Cardiff in 1988 and released by the Court of Appeal in 1992. Doubt was cast over the confessional evidence of Miller, who was interviewed for 13 hours over five days in the presence of a solicitor. The confession was made at the end of the interviews, which were all tape recorded. Evidence was provided that, during the interviews, Miller denied the offence over 300 times. The interviewing officers shouted at him, telling him what he ought to say, and the solicitor who was present during the interviews made no interventions. The Court of Appeal held that the interviews were oppressive, the confession was inadmissible and, with lack of any other evidence, the convictions were quashed. Comment was also made about the failure of the solicitor to intervene when the interview became oppressive. The real killer of Lynette White was convicted in 2003 and 15 members of the original investigation team, including both police officers and police staff, are currently (2010) facing charges of conspiracy to pervert the course of justice.

R v. Heron [1993]

Heron was arrested and charged with the murder of seven-year-old Nikki Allen, who had been found stabbed and beaten to death in Sunderland in 1992. There was some circumstantial evidence but, during a series of interviews, Heron denied the offence 120 times before making a confession. Defence counsel challenged the validity of the taped interviews that contained the confessions, and the judge ruled that seven of the 12 interview tapes were inadmissible because officers had been oppressive during the interview. As a result of this the judge advised the jury to deliver a not guilty verdict. Heron was later taken to the civil court by the mother of the victim and he did not contest a charge of battery of a child resulting in death. He still remains unconvicted of the criminal offence (Bindel, 2006).

Other factors, including psychological reasons why people make false confessions, can also contribute to potential miscarriages of justice, providing further evidence that tape-recorded interviews are not always foolproof.

In addition to the evidential difficulties highlighted, researchers also began to evaluate and assess the performance of the police interviewer. One would have expected, with years of experience at interviewing suspects, that the police would be competent interviewers. Researchers (Moston et al., 1990; Baldwin, 1992, pp15–16) came up with some interesting findings, for example:

- there was an emphasis on obtaining a confession rather than searching for the truth;

- there were criticisms of ineptitude, assumption of guilt, poor interviewing techniques, and unfair, questionable or unprofessional conduct;

- most interviews were carried out by junior officers;

- most officers believed that they were good interviewers despite evidence to the contrary.

The research findings provided a wake-up call for the police service and, as a result, there was a revolution in the training of police interviewers with the introduction of the PEACE course (which provides a standard and ethical methodology for interviewing) and, more recently, tiered interview training delivered through Professionalising the Investigative Process, introduced by ACPO following the Police Reform Act 2002. All police interviewers, ranging from student officers to interview coordinators or advisers, are now required to demonstrate their competency through a nationally recognised qualification framework.

The tape recording of interviews is still the prime means of interviewing a suspect, with visual recording mainly confined to interviewing children and other vulnerable victims/ witnesses, and significant witnesses in serious crime investigations.

Currently, the police service is making the move from analogue to digital recording of interviews, but progress is slow. There are certain difficulties to overcome to ensure the integrity of evidence provided by digital technology, and both training and procurement of the technology also raise significant cost implications.

Technology is now available that takes away the need for tapes, CDs or DVDs. 'Streaming' servers allow police services across the UK to stream their audio or video interviews on to a secure digital platform that can be accessed directly by typists for transcribing interviews, and allow investigating or case review officers to access interviews from any location. Interviews can be monitored remotely in real time and can be digitally bookmarked to find quickly specific sections of an interview (Indico Systems, 2009). Academics have also seized the opportunity to buy into this type of technology. For example, in August 2009, the University of Teesside purchased digital recording technology that will be used to enhance the interview training of Cleveland police student officers, and to assist with international investigative interviewing research.

PRACTICAL TASK

Go to www.publictechnology.net/print.php?sid=21076 and find out more about how this new technology is being used for both policing and academic purposes.

Identification procedures

Technology has been available since 1997 to conduct identification of suspects electronically. Identification suites are very often situated in close proximity to custody areas to facilitate identification procedures with persons in custody. Prior to the intro-duction of electronic identification, public volunteers were required to attend live identification parades. This was very often a time-consuming and costly process, with real difficulties in finding appropriate people with a likeness to the suspect.

To tackle this problem a technological solution known as VIPER (Video Identification Parade Electronic Recording) was designed by West Yorkshire police and a national bureau for VIPER created in Wakefield. The VIPER database holds thousands of video images of suspects and volunteers, and an identification parade can be set up very quickly. In 2003, it was reported that costs had been reduced from £1,500 for a live identification parade to just £150 for a video identification (Number10.gov.uk).

Currently, 32 police organisations within the UK use VIPER and the bureau produces about 50,000 parades per year (National Viper Bureau, 2009). In addition to the cost and resource benefits, the system provides a user-friendly service for victims and witnesses, with the added benefit of being able to conduct a video identification parade on a laptop at home or in hospital.

PRACTICAL TASK

Go to www.viper.police.uk/index.html and find out more about VIPER. Make a list of the benefits the system provides to the public, police, witnesses, victims and suspects.

Fingerprinting of suspects

When a person is arrested for a recordable offence, the police have the power to take and retain fingerprints that are kept on a national database (PACE 1984, s61; Criminal Justice and Police Act 2001, s82). The national fingerprint database is known as IDENT 1, and it provides a fingerprint identification system for the police service in England, Wales and Scotland.

According to the NPIA (2009b), in October 2009 the database contained the following information:

- 8.1 million individuals' tenprints (term used for a set of fingerprints);

- 17.8 million sets of tenprints;

- 1.8 million unidentified fingerprint marks;

- 7.9 million palm prints;

- 156,210 palm marks;

- 4,396 serious crime marks;

- 47,738 scenes of crime identifications over the previous six months.

The technology incorporates an automated search engine known as AFIS (Automated Fingerprint Identification System), which can search the database extremely quickly. Two principal databases are used for searching, one of which contains identity records and the other unidentified crime scene marks.

Most police forces have a fingerprint bureau that can access the national database on a 24-hour basis. Technology continues to be developed and today equipment is available (Livescan) that is able to digitally record an individual's fingerprints, which can be checked immediately against the national database, thus providing a real benefit to policing by means of a speedy and efficient service.

As many as 441 Livescan units are now being used in police custody suites, together with 200 hand-held fingerprint devices that provide mobility and flexibility (NPIA, 2009b). Plans are currently in place to provide the UK Border Agency with access to the database and, in the longer term, a link via the Schengen Information System II (SIS II – an EU-wide system for the collection and exchange of information) will enable checks to be made on a European basis.

Footwear impressions

Modern technology has provided new and enhanced opportunities for investigators to obtain both evidence and intelligence from footwear impressions left at a crime scene. Footwear marks are the second most common evidence type to be left at a crime scene, and they can be used to link a suspect to a crime scene and also link a number of crime scenes together. For example, in 2006 forensic investigators were able to link 25 footwear marks to a series of armed robberies occurring across four counties, resulting in the conviction of six men (www.steria.co.uk, undated).

The Forensic Science Service has now developed and introduced an online footwear coding and detection management system (Footwear Intelligence Technology – FIT), which contains a comprehensive record of tread patterns and code identifications. Previously, the identification and linking of footwear impressions was a slow process, but the new technology now provides the police service with the ability to obtain accurate information in real time and new footwear updates are online within 24 hours.

A shrewd investigator will seize opportunities provided by footwear impressions at a crime scene and will also be aware of this issue when suspects are taken to a custody suite following arrest. Legislation now provides the police service with the power to obtain impressions from the footwear of a person who is arrested for a recordable offence (Serious Organised Crime and Police Act 2005, s118).

C H A P T E R   S U M M A R Y

In this chapter you have been provided with an overview of some of the technology that is used to facilitate and enhance police communications and to provide certain safeguards and security for those detained in police custody.

Opportunities have been provided for further research and a number of contemporaneous issues have been considered, such as the opportunities presented to investigators through scrutiny of police communication systems; crime reporting and public confidence; improved police efficiency through the use of mobile data; the safety of suspects and police accountability in police custody areas; and the tape recording of interviews and false confessions.

The tasks completed should provide stimulus, sources and evidence for completion of NOS and assignments. Further reading and research will provide a more detailed understanding of the impact of technology on police communications and the detention of persons in police custody.

Baldwin, John (1992) *Video Taping Police Interviews with Suspects: An evaluation.* London: Home Office Police Research Group.

Bindel, Julie (2006) There will be no peace for me. *The Guardian*, 11 October. Available online at www.guardian.co.uk/uk/2006/oct/11/ukcrime.features11 (accessed 13 November 2009).

Directgov (2009) *Policing Pledge.* Available online at www.direct.gov.uk/prod_consum_dg/groups/dg_digitalassets/@dg/@en/documents/digitalasset/dg_172297.pdf (accessed 4 December 2009).

Flanagan, Sir Ronnie (2008) *The Review of Policing: Final report.* Available online at http://police.home office.gov.uk/publications/police-reform/Review_of_policing_final_report (accessed 2 November 2009).

Home Office (2008) *From the Neighbourhood to the National: Policing our communities together.* London: The Stationery Office.

Home Office (2009a) *Community Policing: Call handling.* Available online at http://police.homeoffice.gov.uk/community-policing/citizen-focused-policing/call-handling (accessed 27 October 2009).

Home Office (2009b) *Research Development Statistics: Key publications.* Available online at www.homeoffice.gov.uk/rds/recordedcrime1.html (accessed 2 November 2009).

Home Office (2009c) *Operational Policing: Police and Criminal Evidence Act 1984 and accompanying codes of practice.* Available online at: http://police.homeoffice.gov.uk/operational-policing/powers-pace-codes/pace-code-intro (accessed 3 November 2009).

Independent Police Complaints Commission (IPCC) (2009) *Annual Report and Statement of Accounts 2008/09.* London: The Stationery Office. Available online at: www.ipcc.gov.uk/ipcc_annual_report_2008-09_without_accounts.pdf (accessed 6 November 2009).

Indico Systems (2009) *Interview Suite Recording Direct to Server.* Available online at: www.prosecurity zone.com/Customisation/News/Surveillance/Voice_Recording_and_Interview_Suites/Interview_suite_recordings_direct_to_server.asp (accessed 16 November 2009).

Inquest (1998) *Deaths of Black, Minority and Ethnic People in Custody: INQUEST's submission to the Stephen Lawrence Inquiry 1998.* London: Inquest: Available online at: http://inquest.gn.apc.org/pdf/Deaths_of_Black_Minority_and_Ethnic_People_in_Custody_1998.pdf (accessed 6 November 2009).

Leigh, Adrian, Johnson, Graham and Ingram, Alan (2008) *Deaths in Police Custody: Learning the lessons.* London: Police Research Group.

Metropolitan Police (2009) *Metropolitan Police Online Crime Reporting.* Available online at https://online.met.police.uk (accessed 2 November 2009).

Moston, Stephen, Stephenson, Geoffrey and Williamson, Thomas (1990) *Police Interrogation Styles and Suspect Behaviour: Report to the Police Requirements Support Unit.* London: Home Office.

National Policing Improvement Agency (NPIA) (2009a) *Airwave Radio.* Available online at www.npia.police.uk/en/10506.htm (accessed 4 December 2009).

National Policing Improvement Agency (NPIA) (2009b) *Fingerprint Database.* Available online at www.npia.police.uk/en/10504.htm (accessed 1 December 2009).

National Policing Improvement Agency (NPIA) (2009c) *Custody and Case Preparation.* Available online at www.npia.police.uk/en/10515.htm (accessed 4 December 2009).

National Viper Bureau (2009) *What is VIPER?* Available online at www.viper.police.uk/index.html (accessed 17 November 2009).

Newburn, Tim and Hayman, Stephanie (2002) *Policing, Surveillance and Social Control: CCTV and police monitoring of suspects.* Cullompton: Willan.

Number 10.gov.uk (2003) *Video ID Parades Catch Criminals Faster.* Available online at www.number10. gov.uk/Page3275 (accessed 17 November 2009).

Povey, Keith (2001) *Open All Hours: A thematic inspection report on the role of police visibility and accessibility in public reassurance.* London: Her Majesty's Inspectorate of Constabulary.

Radice, Giles (1977) *Mr Liddle Towers.* House of Commons Debate, 12 December 1977, volume 941, cc232–44. Available online at http://hansard.millbanksystems.com/commons/1977/dec/12/mr-liddle-towers (accessed 6 November 2009).

Regan, Simon (1997) The Bridgewater catastrophe, *Scandals in Justice Magazine.* Available online at www.scandals.org/articles/sr970527a.html (accessed 6 November 2009).

Stewart, Robert (1994) *The Police Signal Box: A 100 year history.* Glasgow: University of Strathclyde.

Willis, Carole (1984) *The Tape Recording of Police Interviews with Suspects: An interim report.* London: HMSO.

Willis, Carole, Macleod, John and Naish Peter (1988) *The Tape Recording of Police Interviews with Suspects: A second interim report.* London: HMSO.

www.steria.co.uk (undated) Tracking criminals one step at a time. Available online at www1.steria.co. uk/cms/ukweb.nsf/docs/D7D93F77387609A9802574D400513E1E/$file/Steria%20and%20the%20 Forensic%20Science%20Service.pdf (accessed 1 December 2009).

USEFUL WEBSITES

www.homeoffice.gov.uk (Home Office, with links to crime information, the police and statistics)

www.ipcc.gov.uk (Independent Police Complaints Commission)

www.npia.police.uk (National Policing Improvement Agency)

CASES

R v. Heron [1993] – Leeds Crown Court, November 1993

R v. Paris, Abdullahi and Miller [1992] 97 Cr App R 99

LEGISLATION

Criminal Justice and Police Act 2001

Criminal Procedure and Investigations Act 1996

Police and Criminal Evidence Act 1984

Police Reform Act 2002

Serious Organised Crime and Police Act 2005

10 Technology and the future of policing

CHAPTER OBJECTIVES

By the end of this chapter you should be able to:

- understand how current government and police strategy related to technology and cyber-crime may shape the future of policing within the UK;
- outline some of the potential problems and issues related to the future growth, development and use of technology within policing and the investigation of cyber-crime;
- describe some of the innovative products and systems that are being developed for investigative purposes.

LINKS TO STANDARDS

This chapter provides opportunities for links with the following Skills for Justice, National Occupational Standards (NOS) for Policing and Law Enforcement 2008.

AE1.1   Maintain and develop your own knowledge, skills and competence.
HA1   Manage your own resources.
HA2   Manage your own resources and professional development.

Introduction

In this chapter we will consider what the future may hold for the growth, development and use of technology within policing and the investigation of cyber-crime. We do not have a crystal ball to map out accurately the direction, future and impact of technological innovations within policing, but we can briefly highlight some of the factors that will shape the continuing development and use of technology.

Both the government and the police service have a number of long-term strategies and plans in place that contain aims and objectives related to the development and use of science and technology in policing. The strategies are supported with promises of funding that is critical for technological development and operational use, and they provide direction for senior managers to ensure that resources are made available in support of the strategic aims and objectives. Some of these strategies were highlighted in Chapter 1 and we will briefly explore some of them later in this chapter.

For the investigator, the opportunities and possibilities created by scientific and technological innovation appear to be endless, and we shall evidence this by providing more examples of cutting-edge technology that is currently being developed, or that has recently been introduced into the world of policing.

Cyber-crime: the future

Cyber-crime investigation

What does the future hold with regard to law enforcement and technology, and can we learn from history? When the first motor car was invented, criminals made full use of it to cross jurisdictional boundaries while law enforcement agencies stood still, before eventually catching up and getting some motor cars of their own. Are we going to do, or are we already doing, the same with the computer, the information highway and digital intelligence?

In recent years, the US Department of Homeland Security and various leaders in the computer security community have promoted information and intelligence sharing. In 2004, the *CSI/FBI Computer Crime and Security Survey* detected no increase in the trend to share information about security intrusions (Gordon et al., 2004). In the same year, a parliamentary report from the All Party Internet Group made the following recommendation:

> We also recommend that the police implement suitable procedures that will act as the cyberworld equivalent of taking down the 'Police Line – Do Not Cross' tapes.
>
> (APIG, 2004, p19)

Despite these and other recommendations of a similar nature, there is still a lack of attention to the subject of digital intelligence. For example, there are no references to it currently in 'intelligence-led policing' or the National Intelligence Model, and similarly the 2002 European Commission report, *Creating a Safer Information Society by Improving the Security of Information and Combating Computer-related Crime*, focused on the retention of data by third parties and failed to address, or even mention, law enforcement's retention of data or the intelligence analysis of data. However, the government's *Cyber Security Strategy* does recognise the importance of exploiting digital intelligence (Cabinet Office, 2009, p4), but it is too early to assess whether this will result in positive action and outcomes.

The *ACPO e-Crime Strategy* states that 'e-crime can only be effectively tackled through partnership working, on intelligence, prevention and enforcement (ACPO, 2009, p5), and goes on to make further references to e-crime intelligence. However, as can be seen from this and other comparable studies, investigative guidelines for cyber-crime have a tendency to focus on detection and prosecution. They cover the specialist forensic and investigative work that is required to tackle cyber-crime, but fail to give appropriate attention to the areas of cyber-crime prevention and digital intelligence analysis.

History may provide us with a solution.

CASE STUDY

Who brought down Al Capone, aka 'Scarface': was it Frank J Wilson, the Internal Revenue Service man; George E Q Johnson, the Assistant District Attorney; or Elliot Ness, the prohibition agent? They all played their part but, in real terms, it was none of them – it was a shooting in February 1930 that led to Capone's downfall. The details of it are patchy, and cloaked in secrecy, but what the event did do was trigger the formation of the 'Secret Six', who were six business men from an array of professions. Their aim was to assist law enforcement to take down organised crime and, in particular, Al Capone.

As history tells us, they were successful, because Capone himself admitted it in a statement to the Chicago Herald *in 1932: 'The Secret Six has licked the rackets. They've licked me. They've made it so there's no money in the game' (Barnard, 2003–09).*

Therefore, do we need a modern-day hi-tech six? The previously mentioned ACPO and *Cyber Security* strategies do make reference to such a solution:

> *To build effective partnership relationships with industry, government and academia.*
>
> (ACPO, 2009, p9)

> *an effective response to e-crime requires a broad cross-governmental response involving law enforcement, regulators and national security agencies.*
>
> (Cabinet Office, 2009, p20)

The current approach to cyber-crime in the UK is largely committed to prosecution through the criminal courts, which is somewhat different from that of other countries, whose dependence is on the civil courts. So should we consider:

- the use of private sector controls, requiring organisations to take efficient measures to combat the possibility of cyber-crimes such as security breaches;

- the acknowledgement of the importance of protecting information systems;

- the use of civil remedies to tackle cyber-crime?

Despite these areas of concern, we are moving in the right direction in our fight against cyber-crime. Initially, Skills for Justice identified a suite of National Occupational Standards (NOS) for the police sector, but did not acknowledge the business area of cyber-crime. Now a suite of NOS has been created for cyber-crime and, in 2009, ACPO announced in their *e-Crime Strategy* that they would review and revise the NOS related to e-crime (ACPO, 2009, p11).

REFLECTIVE TASK

Consider the role intelligence has to play in any cyber-crime strategy.

- *Why do you think we are more focused on detection and prosecution?*

- *What are the benefits of an effective cyber-crime intelligence strategy?*

Legislation

Gordon Moore was the co-founder of 'Intel', a global leader in the manufacture of computer chips, and in 1965 he made a visionary statement that is now referred to as 'Moore's law': 'The number of transistors and resistors on a chip doubles every 18 months' (Intel, 2010).

His statement has been exceeded beyond all expectation, with the company expecting to produce a two billion-transistor microprocessor in 2010, providing evidence of the extreme progress of technological development. The principle of Moore's law can be applied to how governments have reacted to the problem of cyber-crime and the concerns that are still evident with legislative programmes.

We have already identified that cyber-crime is committed across cyberspace and does not stop at national borders. More than with any other large-scale crime, the swiftness and flexibility of cyber-crime mean that our existing rules of regulation and legislation quickly become outdated. Such crimes can be perpetrated from anywhere in the world against any computer, and effective action to combat them is necessary at not only a local level but also at an international level. Legislation in most countries has fallen behind, but it needs to maintain the same speed of change as in Moore's law. The international legal systems have achieved some progress by way of the sixth principle on 'Trans-border access to stored computer data' established by G-8 ministers in 1999, commonly known as 'Quick freeze, slow thaw'. This enables law enforcement and judicial bodies to fulfil their procedural obligations under domestic law for the release of information to foreign law enforcement or judicial officials without risking the loss of critical data (Putnam and Elliott, 2000, p64).

However, the detection and punishment of hi-tech crime is highly likely to remain problematic. This type of crime is perceived to suffer from an increased tendency towards 'legislative dependence'; in other words, a long period of time elapsing between innovations in criminal enterprise and the response of the state and law enforcement agencies. Technology, and as a result digital crime, develops and changes very rapidly and it takes years for legislation to be enacted, by which time the crime and criminal will have developed a different form of modus operandi. As a consequence, there are those who say that many digital crimes and criminals cannot be dealt with appropriately under current legislation and, unfortunately, this is not likely to change in the near future.

REFLECTIVE TASK

Consider how the legislative problem could be overcome to keep pace with technological development. To assist with your reflection, access the following online sources:

- *http://www.itu.int/ITU-D/cyb/cybersecurity/projects/cyberlaw.html – provides a link to an American toolkit for cyber-crime legislation (April 2009) that seeks global harmonisation of legal frameworks and international cooperation;*

- *http://www.cybercrimelaw.net/documents/cybercrime_history.pdf – provides a link to a paper presenting a summary of the story of the global harmonising of computer crime and cybercrime legislation from the very first efforts in the late 1970s to initiatives in Geneva in 2008.*

Government and cyber-crime

On 26 August 1768, when Captain James Cook set sail for Australia, it took 2 years and 320 days before he returned to describe what he found there. Yesterday, on 15 June 2009, 20 hours of new content were posted on YouTube every minute, 494 exabytes* of information were transferred seamlessly across the globe, over 2.6 billion mobile minutes were exchanged across Europe, and millions of enquiries were made using a Google algorithm.

(Lord Carter, cited in BIS/DMCS, 2009, p3)

(Note: * 1 exabyte = 1 billion gigabytes.)

Lord Carter's eloquent statement provides an insight into the nature of the digital revolution that the UK and indeed the world is experiencing. The government has reacted to the challenge by putting in place legislation, regulation, policy, practices and strategies to manage the digital revolution and to reap the benefits that it brings.

Cyber-crime has become a global issue and remains a difficult challenge for both government and law enforcement agencies, and the future will be shaped by the effectiveness of the design and delivery of government strategy. Two of the key government strategies are:

- *Digital Britain*;

- the *Cyber Security Strategy*.

Digital Britain

The government paper, *Digital Britain*, was published in June 2009 and provides a programme of action to:

- deliver an effective modern communications infrastructure built on new digital technologies;

- enable Britain to be a global centre for the creative industries in a digital age;

- ensure that people have the capability and skills to flourish in a digital economy and that all can participate in a digital society;

- modernise and improve services through digital procurement and digital delivery of public services.

(adapted from BIS/DCMS, 2009, p1)

The programme sets out a number of ambitions such as 'to secure the UK's position as one of the world's leading digital knowledge economies' (BIS/DCMS, 2009, p7). Whether the UK is capable of achieving this ambition remains to be seen, but a clear message of intent is being delivered by the government and what is happening now could be described as a new age industrial revolution.

A section of the strategy relates directly to digital security and safety, and aspires to enable all people to work online with confidence and safety. There are many threats to Internet users, such as:

- being exposed to harmful and offensive material;

- the spread of malicious gossip and libel;

- scams to obtain money by deception and to steal identities;

- individuals' privacy being compromised;

- vulnerable people being led to harm themselves or others;

- cyber attacks destroying systems that are critical to government, business and individuals.

It is recognised that use of the Internet cannot be totally risk free, but the government has a duty to ensure that any risks are minimised. Their vision of a 'digital Britain' is currently being realised, opening up a world of opportunity for all and presenting new challenges to the investigator that will require significant funding, extensive training, sufficient resources, and an ability to be able to quickly respond to the ever-changing nature of digital technology and cyber-crime.

The *Cyber Security Strategy*

The *Cyber Security Strategy* sets out the government's plans to achieve safety, security and resilience in cyberspace, and has three objectives:

- to reduce risk from the UK's use of cyber space;

- to exploit opportunities in cyberspace;

- to improve knowledge, capabilities and decision making.

(adapted from Cabinet Office, 2009, p4)

Exploiting opportunities includes the gathering of intelligence on criminals, terrorists and states for espionage, influence or warfare purposes, and is recognised as being a key area in tackling the problems of crime and terrorism.

Two new cyber structures were introduced in September 2009 to support the strategy:

- **Office of Cyber Security (OCS)**: based in the Cabinet Office and responsible for delivery of the *Cyber Security Strategy*;

- **Cyber Security Operations Centre (CSOC)**: a multi-agency unit based at GCHQ, Cheltenham, and responsible for monitoring developments in cyberspace, analysing trends and improving technical response coordination to cyber-incidents.

Both the OCS and CSOC will work in conjunction with a number of key agencies, such as ACPO, the Security Service, the Centre for the Protection of the National Infrastructure (CPNI), the Joint Terrorism Analysis Centre (JTAC), Government Communications Head-quarters (GCHQ), the Serious Organised Crime Agency (SOCA) and others.

REFLECTIVE TASK

Go to www.cabinetoffice.gov.uk/reports/cyber_security.aspx, download the Cyber Security Strategy *and read about the eight workstreams that the OCS is responsible for (pages 17–20).*

Workstream 8 makes specific reference to the prevention of e-crime and bringing offenders to justice. Identify which agencies have a strategic or operational role, and consider the implications of, and viability of, the cross-governmental approach alluded to.

The strategy clearly identifies intelligence as a key area to exploit and you may have identified that both a cross-governmental and multi-agency approach will be required to maximise intelligence opportunities in cyberspace.

Government and technology

In Chapter 1, we highlighted the important role of science and technology in any criminal justice strategy and briefly mentioned the current *Science and Innovation Strategy 2009–12*, in which crime and policing feature as two of the six priority areas.

> *There is an ever-increasing pace of change in technology. It is vital that we keep pace with such changes, to use technologies to protect the public, to capture the perpetrators of crimes and ensure that we stay one step ahead of those who wish to subvert our security and way of life.*

(Home Office, 2009a, p1)

This quotation is taken from the foreword of the strategy and captures the essence of why technological development is so important for the security and safety of the UK. Table 10.1 provides a summary of some of the areas that the strategy sets out to tackle in the future through the use of science and technology.

Table 10.1 Technological solutions for tackling crime in the future

The problem	Technological solution
Gun and knife crime	• Electronic detection of weapons. • Development of stand-off (at a distance) and hand-held technology.
Drugs and alcohol	• 'Low-Angle X-ray Scatter' project, providing the ability to detect drugs more quickly and effectively. • Developing the technique of 'surface enhanced Raman spectroscopy' to improve its capability for roadside drug detection.
Organised crime	• Working with industry to develop improved covert surveillance technologies. • Increased use of biometrics, such as facial and iris recognition, and electronic fingerprinting.
Designing out crime	• Developing innovations to help make personal electronics more crime-proof.
Major crime	• CCTV – developing a 'universal viewer' (capable of viewing all digital file formats) and developing systems and technology to investigate more effectively captured CCTV footage. • Developing facial recognition technology.
Evidence and intelligence capture	• Development and use of unmanned aerial vehicles (surveillance drones).

Counter-terrorism

The government also has a *Science and Technology Strategy for Countering International Terrorism* (Home Office, 2009b), recognising that modern technology has been exploited by terrorists and that science and technology have a key part to play in counter-terrorism work. The strategy attempts to consider likely scientific and technological impacts on terrorism up to the year 2020.

Terrorists have taken advantage of communications technology to spread violent extremist ideology and propaganda to a global audience, and have also been able to facilitate fundraising, recruitment, training and operational planning. The new technology allows some terrorists to plan operations more securely and there is evidence available that terrorist groups have attempted to find materials through use of the Internet, in order to develop chemical, biological, radiological and nuclear weapons.

> While technology has provided powerful new tools, techniques and tactics in support of the terrorist agenda, it is also a key element in our response. Success in delivering relevant science, innovation and technology is vital.
>
> (Home Office, 2009b, p9)

PRACTICAL TASK

Go to http://security.homeoffice.gov.uk/news-publications/publication-search/science-technology/Science-Technology-strategy/index.html and find out how the government intends to develop and use technology to combat the threat of terrorism. Identify what measures are planned that will assist the terrorist investigator.

Implications for policing and technology

Government strategy and associated funding are designed to steer the police service in a direction that will maximise scientific and technological opportunities. The threat of terrorism is real, organised crime continues to provide substantial challenges for law enforcement agencies, and locally crime and disorder, road safety and community safety need to be effectively tackled and managed.

In Chapter 1 we identified a range of police science and technology organisations that are at the forefront of developing cutting-edge technology to ensure that the police service and other law enforcement agencies are able to meet the challenges of the modern world effectively. Investigators today need the knowledge and skills to tackle cyber-crime and keep one step ahead of the criminal, and also need to be provided with the cutting-edge technology.

REFLECTIVE TASK

Consider the impact of these cuts for the police service.

- *Where are the savings going to be made, and is it possible that plans for the development, implementation and use of modern technological solutions for policing and the investigator could be compromised?*

- *How can the right balance be achieved between human and technological resources?*

What the police service does have now is an *e-Crime Strategy* and a Police Central e-Crime Unit (PCeU), which will contribute to making the police service within the UK fit for purpose in this cyber age (see Chapters 1 and 5).

An ACPO e-Crime Committee, made up of both senior police officers and agencies involved in e-crime, provides an integrated national approach. The committee is responsible for a number of key initiatives that will contribute to improving both police and law enforcement agencies' responses, in order to tackle effectively the problems of e-crime. Members of the committee are responsible for nine strands of business and each strand has a defined remit with a number of dynamic key activities:

- a central/regional e-crime structure;

- the Olympics;

- training, recruitment and retention;

- regional e-crime units;

- forensics;

- legal issues;

- prevention;

- increasing knowledge for action;

- research and development.

(adapted from ACPO, 2009, p10)

To find out more about the above nine strands of business, go to pages 10–13 of the ACPO e-Crime Strategy *at www.acpo.police.uk/asp/policies/data/Ecrime%20Strategy% 20Website%20Version.pdf.*

New horizons and investigative challenges

The pace of change within the digital revolution continues unabated. The challenge for policing and investigators has already been highlighted, together with the opportunities it brings. New and exciting scientific and technological innovations are constantly being introduced, and below are a number of examples of some of the innovative products that are being developed for investigative purposes.

Case management technology

NICHE Technology UK has produced a records management system that provides end-to-end management of an incident. Data are entered only once on to a digital system, from the initial report right through to the electronic court file, which provides links with both the Crown Prosecution Service (CPS) and the courts. The system can record and store the initial report, intelligence, details of property, statements, scanned paper exhibits, and photographs. North Wales Police have reported a 42 per cent reduction in case file management (*The Investigator*, 2009a, p32).

Chemistry and smell

The University of Tennessee, USA, funded by the Federal Bureau of Investigation's (FBI) Counterterrorism and Forensic Science Research Unit, is developing a lightweight analyser for buried remains and decomposition odour recognition (LABRADOR). This is a portable device that can be taken to major disasters or crime scenes to detect quickly a buried human body (*The Investigator*, 2009a, p40). It will also have the capability to determine the time elapsed since death at the crime scene, providing the investigator with early critical information to develop an effective investigative strategy.

There are 450 chemical compounds released by a decaying body and the technology is designed to capture and recognise some of these compounds. When patented in 2006, other benefits of the technology were recognised, such as the possibility of incorporating the technology into security systems linked to surveillance cameras, in order to detect intruders through odours (WIPO, 2006). The use of smell and the detection of chemical compounds are opening new frontiers for the investigator.

Facial recognition

The development of facial recognition technology is providing more opportunities for investigators and can be linked to video surveillance systems to find, identify and track a face in a crowd or at a specific location. The technology, also known as smart CCTV, has been available for some years and was introduced in the borough of Newham, London, in 1998. In 2001, it was linked to a central Metropolitan Police control room and the CCTV system in Birmingham city centre (Rogerson, 2002).

In June 2001, 100,000 people attending the Super Bowl in Florida had their faces scanned by facial recognition technology in a search for wanted criminals. The technology made 19 identifications, most being false alarms, and was considered by some to be a failure (Marshall, 2007).

This raises the question, 'Does the technology work?' In October 2009, it was announced at a conference in London that the FBI would not be using facial recognition because the algorithms do not exist yet to provide reliable verification of identity (Moss, 2009). Effective facial recognition relies on clear high-resolution images that are not always captured by video surveillance systems.

In November 2006, a project to develop a Facial Imaging National Database (FIND), using images of suspects captured while in custody, was started but, due to funding difficulties, came to an end in March 2008. The NPIA is now responsible for assessing and developing the potential of automated face recognition and a facility now exists to store captured images on the PNC. During the FIND project, a police standard for capturing facial images was introduced, entitled *Police Standard for Still Image Capture and Data Interchange of Facial/Mugshot and Scar, Mark & Tattoo Images*. The idea is to produce quality images for facial mapping and facial recognition technologies. One of the aims of the national database is to give the police service immediate access to images for both intelligence and investigative purposes.

The technology that we are likely to see in the future comprises mobile data devices that provide police officers with immediate access to any image on a police national database, and technology with the capability of recognising facial images through the use of CCTV and ANPR linked into national image databases. 'Behavioural matching' technology is also being developed – cameras will be able to pick out odd behaviour such as a thief loitering around a parked motor vehicle.

In Chapter 6 we have already considered the spectre of 'Big Brother' and the surveillance society. Consider further the human rights and privacy implications of these planned innovations. Are we going beyond what is reasonable for national safety and security? To help with your reflections consider the following three articles, which can be found online.

- *www.guardian.co.uk/uk/2008/mar/19/ukcrime.humanrights*

- *www.marcvallee.co.uk/ft/FT_171009_page3.pdf*

- *www.timesonline.co.uk/tol/comment/columnists/guest_contributors/article5504534.ece*

ACPO is planning to introduce the first portable readers for police officers by March 2010 that will be capable of iris and facial recognition and of reading identity cards, passports, bank and credit cards, and fingerprints (infosecurity.com, 2009).

Police National Database

Sir Michael Bichard, in his 2004 report following the murder of two schoolgirls in Soham in 2002, recommended that the police service should develop a national intelligence system (Home Office, 2004, p13). You may be surprised that, even with the range and sophistication of technology available today, the police service still does not have a national intelligence database.

In the past, the police service has used a variety of IT applications for the recording and storage of intelligence, with no capability for electronically sharing intelligence on a national basis. The NPIA is responsible for developing a Police National Database (PND) and the first phase of the project is expected during the early part of 2010. The database will allow the police service to share, access and search local information electronically, providing immediate access to up-to-date information and intelligence from any police organisation linked to the database (NPIA, 2010).

Consider the benefits of a national intelligence database and make a list of the advantages and disadvantages that it may bring for the police service, the community, and the individual.

Reveal Laser

The police in Nanaimo, Vancouver Island, Canada, are now using a revolutionary piece of technology known as the 'Reveal Laser'. A green laser light can see writing through envelopes, can detect trace evidence through as many as 24 layers of paint, and can more effectively identify fingerprints, footwear impressions, fibres and other biological evidence that may have been missed previously in a crime scene search. It is designed to cause less damage to potential evidence during a crime scene search, to find more evidence at a crime scene, and to provide a much faster search (*The Investigator*, 2009b, p27).

The virtual world

Second Life and World of Warcraft are two online virtual worlds enjoyed by many on the Internet mainly for leisure purposes; however, within Second Life participants can purchase virtual currency known as 'Linden dollars' to trade and operate businesses online. The website is unregulated and has already been targeted by criminals to launder money (Simpson, 2009, p9).

A case in China involved an individual who reported that his $1,500 dragon sword had been stolen from his online 'World of Warcraft' account. The police did not take the report seriously until the individual concerned found the online thief and murdered him (Simpson, 2009, p9).

These are two good examples of the changing nature of crime, requiring effective responses from law enforcement agencies and new challenges for the investigator in a virtual world.

Where to next?

As stated previously, the possibilities with science and technology are endless and we will continue to be both amazed and challenged by innovative developments. The government in 2010 has now finally woken up to the realities of cyber-crime and has put in place plans that should take the UK forward and ready to face effectively the challenges it will bring.

The Olympic Games 2012

The UK has the privilege of hosting the Olympic Games in 2012 and the Metropolitan Police will be responsible for policing the event. Technology will play a key role in providing security for the games, which have in the past attracted criminal elements and have always been a target for terrorists.

The NPIA is one of the key strategic partners in helping to deliver a safe, secure and resilient 2012 Olympic and Paralympic Games. We have already identified in Chapter 1 that the NPIA is responsible for a range of key scientific and technological projects for the police service, and some of these projects will be critical for the successful policing of the Games.

REFLECTIVE TASK

Go to http://community.iss4ps.police.uk/cs/files/folders/124/download.aspx and download the NPIA Olympics Catalogue. *Identify the technological solutions that the NPIA is offering for the policing of the Games and consider how important this technology is for both security and safety at the Olympic and Paralympic Games.*

Despite the economic downturn, the Games will be given some priority by the government and the technological projects will need to be delivered on time.

The space age

Satellite technology provides sophisticated global communications and incredible surveillance capabilities, but what are the possibilities for the future? Picture the following as a potential scenario for achieving safer roads and reducing car crime in the future.

To gain access to a motor vehicle, biometric technology (facial, eye or fingerprint recognition) will be used to allow the driver access. Before the engine can be started, the driver will have to activate a device that will test for drugs or alcohol. If a driver is breaking a speed limit, intelligent satellite technology (the same principle as a 'sat nav' device) will communicate with the engine to bring it down to the correct speed.

This technology is available and research is currently being conducted that may result in this scenario becoming reality for us all in years to come (see Chapter 8).

C H A P T E R   S U M M A R Y

In this chapter we have identified how science and technology have been embraced by government, law enforcement agencies and investigators, in order to meet the challenges and maximise the opportunities of a global digital revolution.

We have briefly examined a number of key strategies relating to science, technology and cyber-crime that will shape the future of how technology is developed and implemented. From a policing perspective, considerable resources will be required to support the momentum of scientific and technological development, and the strategies will be expected to produce positive outcomes, such as digital safety for all, and the prevention, reduction and detection of crime.

The importance of intelligence has been discussed and how the focus of governments and law enforcement agencies has until recently neglected this issue. It has been pointed out how organised criminals and terrorists have quickly reaped the benefits of the digital revolution and how any strategy developed to tackle these threats effectively must have a robust intelligence element.

A number of exciting and cutting-edge technologies have been highlighted, evidencing the growth of innovation within policing, and we have considered how some of this technology has led to public concerns about privacy and civil liberties.

The tasks in this chapter, together with others throughout the book, should have provided you with stimulus, sources and evidence for completion of NOS and assignments. Further academic reading and research will provide you with a more detailed understanding of the use of science and technology within policing for investigative purposes, and will be especially necessary for second- and third-year higher education (HE) students, who will need to provide evidence of wider research and analysis to attain a first-class grade.

REFERENCES

All Party Internet Group (APIG) (2004) *Revision of the Computer Misuse Act: Report of an inquiry by the All Party Internet Group*. London: APIG. Available online at www.apcomms.org.uk/apig/archive/activities-2004/computer-misuse-inquiry/CMAReportFinalVersion1.pdf (accessed 18 January 2010).

Association of Chief Police Officers (ACPO) (2009) *ACPO e-Crime Strategy*. London: ACPO.

Barnard, Thomas (2003–09) *The Secret Six*. Available online at www.thomasbarnard.com/Articles/secretsix.htm (accessed 18 January 2010).

Cabinet Office (2009) *Cyber Security Strategy of the United Kingdom: Safety, security and resilience in cyber space.* Norwich: The Stationery Office.

Department for Business Innovation & Skills/Department for Culture, Media and Sport (BIS/DCMS) (2009) *Digital Britain: Final report*. Norwich: The Stationery Office.

Gordon, Lawrence, Loeb, Martin, Lucyshyn, William and Richardson, Robert (2004) *CSI/FBI Computer Crime and Security Survey*. Available online at www.securitymanagement.com/archive/library/CSI_FBI_ComputerCrime0904.pdf (accessed 18 January 2010).

Home Office (2004) *The Bichard Inquiry Report.* London: The Stationery Office.

Home Office (2009a) *Science and Innovation Strategy 2009–12.* London: Home Office Science and Research Group.

Home Office (2009b) *United Kingdom's Science and Technology Strategy for Countering International Terrorism.* London: Home Office.

Infosecurity.com (2009) ACPO seeks ID card readers, 19 October. Available online at www.infosecurity-magazine.com/view/4635/acpo-seeks-id-card-readers (accessed 25 January 2010).

Intel (2010) *Moore's Law.* Available online at http://www.intel.com/technology/mooreslaw (accessed 1 February 2010).

The Investigator (2009a) Integrated operational systems. *The Investigator*, September/October. Available online at www.the-investigator.co.uk (accessed 22 January 2010).

The Investigator (2009b) Laser will reveal destroyed hidden evidence. *The Investigator*, December. Available online at www.the-investigator.co.uk (accessed 25 January 2010).

Marshall, Patrick (2007) We can see clearly now: after an early black eye, face recognition might finally be ready for prime time. *Government Computer News* (Virginia, USA), 4 June. Available online at www.itl.nist.gov/iad/News/FaceRecog3.html (accessed 1 February 2010).

Moss, David (2009) The Home Office's broken biometrics. *The Guardian*, 1 November. Available online at www.guardian.co.uk/commentisfree/libertycentral/2009/nov/01/biometrics-home-office (accessed 25 January 2010).

National Policing Improvement Agency (NPIA) (2010) *Police National Database*. Available online at www.npia.police.uk/en/8495.htm (accessed 25 January 2010).

Putnam, Tonya and Elliott, David (2000) *International Responses to Cyber Crime*. Available online at http://media.hoover.org/documents/0817999825_35.pdf (accessed 1 February 2010).

Rogerson, Simon (2002) Smart CCTV. *IMIS Journal*, 12(1), February. Available online at www.ccsr.cse.dmu.ac.uk/resources/general/ethicol/Ecv12no1.html (accessed (22 January 2010).

Simpson, Christopher (2009) Applying cutting edge technologies to criminal investigations: conference review. *The Investigator*, November/December. Available online at www.the-investigator.co.uk (accessed 25 January 2010).

World Intellectual Property Organization (WIPO) (2006) *Method and Apparatus for Detecting Humans and Human Remains* (WO/2006/078255). Available online at www.wipo.int/pctdb/ja/wo.jsp?WO=2006 078255&IA=US2005002789&DISPLAY=DESC (accessed 22 January 2010).

USEFUL WEBSITES

www.acpo.police.uk (Association of Chief Police Officers)

www.homeoffice.gov.uk (Home Office, with links to crime information, the police and statistics)

www.number10.gov.uk (the official site of the Prime Minister's Office, containing links to news on crime and technology)

www.parliament.uk (UK Parliament website, which has links to legislation)

www.police.homeoffice.gov.uk (combines all the police-related information, support and guidance published by the Home Office)

www.the-investigator.co.uk (*The Investigator* is an online magazine carrying articles on the latest technology for crime investigation)

Index

Text within task boxes has also been included in the following index, where relevant.

W

web crawlers 26
web pages/sites 27, 31
   see also Internet

White, Lynette 155
witnesses, specialist/expert 72–3
World Wide Web (WWW) 17–18
   see also Internet